SOVEREIGN UNDER GOD

America: We The People
One Nation, 50 Republics

SOVEREIGN UNDER GOD

Rules For Radical Liberty:
Think And Be Free

Paul Phaneuf

America: We The People
One Nation, 50 Republics

SOVEREIGN UNDER GOD

Rules For Radical Liberty:
Think And Be Free

Paul Phaneuf

Copyright Notice

Contents

Paul Phaneuf

Contents

Foreword

"Without morals a republic cannot subsist any length of time; they therefore who are decrying the Christian religion, whose morality is so sublime and pure (and) which insures to the good eternal happiness, are undermining the solid foundation of morals, the best security for the duration of free governments."

Charles Carroll[1]

The spirit of resistance to government is so valuable on certain occasions that I wish it to be always kept alive.

Thomas Jefferson

The following is quoted in its entirety:

"Have you ever wondered what happened to the 56 men who signed the Declaration of Independence?

Five signers were captured by the British as traitors, and tortured before they died. Twelve had their homes ransacked and burned. Two lost their sons serving in the Revolutionary Army; another had two sons captured. Nine of the 56 fought and died from wounds or hardships of the Revolutionary War. They signed and they pledged their lives, their fortunes, and their sacred honor. What kind of men were they?

Twenty-four were lawyers and jurists. Eleven were merchants, nine were farmers and large plantation owners; men of means, well educated. But they signed the Declaration of Independence knowing full well that the penalty would be death if they were captured.

Paul Phaneuf

Carter Braxton of Virginia, a wealthy planter and trader, saw his ships swept from the seas by the British Navy. He sold his home and properties to pay his debts, and died in rags. Thomas McKeam was so hounded by the British that he was forced to move his family almost constantly. He served in the Congress without pay, and his family was kept in hiding. His possessions were taken from him, and poverty was his reward.

Vandals or soldiers looted the properties of Dillery, Hall, Clymer, Walton, Gwinnett, Heyward, Ruttledge, and Middleton. At the battle of Yorktown, Thomas Nelson, Jr. noted that the British General Cornwallis had taken over the Nelson home for his headquarters. He quietly urged General George Washington to open fire. The home was destroyed, and Nelson died bankrupt.

Francis Lewis had his home and properties destroyed. The enemy jailed his wife, and she died within a few months. John Hart was driven from his wife's bedside as she was dying. Their 13 children fled for their lives. His fields and his gristmill were laid to waste. For more than a year he lived in forests and caves, returning home to find his wife dead and his children vanished. A few weeks later, he died from exhaustion and a broken heart. Norris and Livingston suffered similar fates.

Such were the stories and sacrifices of the American Revolution. These were not wild-eyed, rabble-rousing ruffians. They were soft-spoken men of means and education. They had security, but they valued liberty more."

Introduction

"What luck for rulers that men do not think."
Adolf Hitler

"Those people who will not be governed by God will be ruled by tyrants."
William Penn

If you have ever pondered over how intrusive government is in every level of your life, this book is for you. Try to imagine any action you want to take in your public or private life that is not regulated, monitored, restricted, or taxed, and about which you do not have to answer to some government official to obtain permission, permit, license, certification, or whatever term is applied. It's not easy. In fact it's nearly impossible.

Imagine how a civilized country could function if government did not micro manage everything. Would all things grind to a halt? Has government convinced you that if it were not for meddlesome bureaucrats our whole civilization would fall apart?

Would it surprise you to hear that the most efficient, prosperous, happy, and secure nation would be based on a model of wide liberty? That it is what the Founders envisioned? That it is this vision which propelled us to the creation of a prosperous middle class to an extent never before achieved by any nation? That it is, in fact, a Godly vision? Do you believe that this is what we now have?

Paul Phaneuf

This book is a treatise based on my own journey to discover, and my subsequent efforts to encourage the mindset that a free people absolutely must cultivate to ensure a free society. These thoughts were not conceived by me. They were given to me by great men, great books, and a great God. Herein I express my understanding of freedom and its roots in the Christian faith based on my studies of history, philosophy, the Judeo Christian scriptures and the writings of the Founders of this once great country.

I have written it because I believe that while our nation is still powerful and truly exceptional in our aspirations and potential, we are no longer great. We have compromised with the same dark and discredited forces that have consistently destroyed earlier civilizations. Who among "We the People" want these United States of America to be anything less than great? Who among us who love freedom want to leave to our posterity the tyrannical monster we have allowed to breed and grow? Sadly, and shockingly, there are public servants in office today who work ceaselessly to undermine rather than enhance the strength of our nation.

While many contemporary issues are referenced for the sake of context, this book is not intended to be a comprehensive analysis of the state of our union, nor is it a minute examination of many of the particular issues and problems that plague us, whether internal or external, or whether self inflicted or imposed upon us by others.

What I am sharing is my own mindset as a man who would be free in a nation that was founded upon the principle of God-granted individual liberty. Regardless of one's religious affiliation, the phrase "endowed by our Creator" speaks directly to the origin of our Liberty[2]. It is a broad subject which I have attempted to crystallize into a coherent, pragmatic, and actionable paradigm, and I take responsibility for any shortcomings.

In a very practical sense, as we have all heard, perception is reality. To a certain extent we see what we want to see and hear what we want to hear. We must be vigilant to examine our convictions and conclusions so that what we believe aligns with what actually is.

In our time we must have the wisdom and courage to admit that what we now have in America is not true liberty. It is the appearance of liberty. Liberty has become like a cheap piece of furniture that is nothing more than inexpensive particle board covered with a thin veneer of cherry wood. The tiniest scratch reveals that it is not what it appears to be.

Within these pages you will read the argument for true liberty and the warning call that we are at risk and that genuine freedom is in its death throes here in America. I encourage you to consider whether you are hearing truths that you can appropriate and act upon, even if you do not agree with everything you read in these pages.

This is not an evangelical polemic, but I am a Christian and it is the place from which I start. I understand and celebrate that each of us are free to believe what we choose to believe, and ask only that you take the initiative to actually dig deep within yourself, and confirm that you are comfortable that you know who you are. The point of this book is to discuss exactly what that means and why it is important.

This is not to say that you must be a Christian to be a free American. You will judge for yourself. Nevertheless, is it not profound that no other nation has ever been founded on the belief that rights are inherent to the nature of man[3], granted by their Creator, unalienable?[4] In order to appreciate the ideas in this book, you do not have to accept the Judeo Christian principles as good or bad, right or wrong; most people acknowledge that these principles were present in the minds of the Founders when they thought through how they were going to establish a new Republic.

My argument begins with the premise that you and I are sovereign beings. While that is immensely significant, our sovereignty is tempered and framed by the sober reality that we are nevertheless not The Sovereign Being. Whatever your understanding is of the origin of humankind, or whatever your belief about what the source of the universe itself may be, very few of us are under the delusion that we are ourselves The Supreme Being.

Ours is a substantive but limited sovereignty, but it is limited by our allegiance to that which is superior to us, not by that which is inferior to us. This is a significant insight if one follows this thought process through to its unavoidable conclusions. We live our lives according to a hierarchy of values. For the sake of an arbitrary example, most of us would agree that it is good to be charitable; it is better to be generous; it is wrong to be unkind; it is worse to murder, etc.

This concept of a hierarchy of values is relevant when we analyze our relationship with the government that is supposed to protect our liberties. It is my hope that together we can consider the importance of these distinctions in these pages.

Regardless of our differences, our understanding of ultimate reality is such that most of us sense that in some way we proceed from some being or force, or at least sequentially come after it in time. What this means is that most of us do believe that some Force or Being existed before us.

Most of us would also concede that from each of us flows energy that is manifested in our lives as creative thoughts, which through our efforts become artwork, products, institutions, and whatever else exists because we have acted. Simply put: we think, we act, and we create.

Here is an important precept to consider: the fact that we exist makes us logically antecedent to that which we create. Like our own origin and the notion that something came before us, we exist prior to anything we make. This may sound simplistic, but it has consequences if true. It means we are therefore prior to and sovereign over and by nature superior to that which we make. The clay does not tell the potter what it shall be.[5] It does not demote him. It does not scold him. It does not acquire authority over him of its own accord. The potter does not bow to the clay he has molded.

A brief work such as this cannot be comprehensive for the subject is vast. At any point, at every point, the reader is urged to do his or her own research and thinking. This is critical. The purpose of this book is to provoke thought. Blind faith is for fools. Even God invites us to "reason together."[6]

Hopefully the attempt will be worthwhile for my effort to write it and yours to read it. If some are piqued to consider matters they may not have otherwise addressed or have perhaps avoided, I will be grateful and satisfied. If some are spurred to greater action or involvement in the work of our Republic, then I would be elated. If, because my own journey has included the spiritual, this is encouraging to you, then I would be blessed.

Many argue, perhaps justifiably in this day and age, that we are a secular nation. In 2012, the White House was occupied by the first President of these United States of

America to assert that "we are no longer a Christian nation." This statement suggests that even to him, if we "no longer" are "a Christian nation," then that implies that we once were.

This is an ominous sign and a sorry admission if he means we have strayed from our values. It is dire if he means we have abandoned them. It is catastrophic if he means that we have rejected them. One must ask, in lieu of what?

Perhaps, based on the libertine and selfish nature of our culture, we must admit that we have strayed from our roots. It is indisputable that the Founders wanted no establishment of Religion by the federal government; nevertheless, that they were committed to the principles that the Christian faith professed cannot reasonably be denied.

So what claim is made in these pages? It is that like me, you have a paradigm, a worldview, a notion of how the world works. We have either consciously constructed it by ourselves through reflection or study, or we have subconsciously absorbed it from our education or environment. If we are not sure of how we have come to our beliefs, then it is time to determine that for ourselves, in our own lives.

To ask the question on a personal level, when you are who you are and you think and act, where do you "come from?" What is your worldview? Examine it. Question it. Understand it. Claim it. Defend it. Without that discipline, we cannot know ourselves, nor can we truly affect our culture.

You do not have to adopt my worldview or even that of the Founders' to perform an honest intellectual inquiry for the purpose of gaining an understanding of their perceptions and purposes. At the end of this work, you will find resources that you can study and come to your own conclusions if you haven't already.

Accept the following fact, and pardon this unequivocal warning: freedom from government and tyranny is not an accident. In fact, in the history of humankind, freedom is an aberration. It can disappear virtually overnight.

One may ask; how do we begin such an undertaking? Let us begin with some basics. At all points I have found that I must begin with myself. For each of us, the universe begins at where and who we are. It all starts from within, so let us consider. What is the significance of freedom to who we are and how we live in this world? Why does it even matter?

PART ONE

INNER MAN

"These are the times that try men's souls. The summer soldier and the sunshine patriot will, in this crisis, shrink from the service of their country; but he that stands it now, deserves the love and thanks of man and woman. Tyranny, like hell, is not easily conquered; yet we have this consolation with us, that the harder the conflict, the more glorious the triumph. What we obtain too cheap, we esteem too lightly: it is dearness only that gives every thing its value. Heaven knows how to put a proper price upon its goods; and it would be strange indeed if so celestial an article as freedom should not be highly rated."

Thomas Paine

"Liberty not only means that the individual has both the opportunity and the burden of choice; it also means that he must bear the consequences of his actions and will receive praise or blame for them. Liberty and responsibility are inseparable."

Friedrich Hayek, ***THE CONSTITUTION OF LIBERTY*** *(1960)*

1 - Where Does Freedom Begin?

*"Men occasionally stumble over truth; most of them pick them-
selves up and hurry off as if nothing had happened."*
Winston Churchill

*In disquisitions of every kind there are certain primary truths,
or first principles, upon which all subsequent reasoning must
depend.*
Alexander Hamilton, Federalist No. 20

*Stand upright, speak thy thoughts, declare the truth thou hast,
that all may share; be bold, proclaim it everywhere: They only live
who dare.*
Lewis Morris

All that you will find in this manuscript regarding
freedom is predicated upon what history has found to be
an inescapable reality:

no man will long remain free who does not understand
what freedom is;

freedom will have no meaning or fundamental value to
him if he has not thought through and cannot defend to
himself or others why he is free by virtue of his nature;

and one's defense of freedom will not be possible until
he knows who he is, knows what he believes, and knows
why he believes it.

Freedom begins in the mind and before it can be lived
it must be known.

Paul Phaneuf

Thinking is that quality of the mind from which proceed all impulses to purposeful action. A man may react impulsively without thinking, but to anticipate, to be proactive, to respond, to conclude, to deduce, to aspire to be wise requires a mind that is established in reason, embedded in principle, and practiced in the science and art of contemplative reflection. In other words, a man must be able to observe his own thoughts in order to honestly understand and evaluate if his thinking is sound.

To trust one's own mind demands humility; without it one will not admit to error and cannot stand corrected and improved. To trust one's own conclusions requires that one has sought to learn and to progress. Without this attitude, one has no right to trust himself although he may have enjoyed good fortune; for corrections to self must be viewed as desirable and are best absorbed in measured doses. Adjustments that are frequent and less traumatic make the process of acquired learning fruitful and yield insights that are satisfying instead of dreadful. For as it is observed by all, the higher the rise, the deeper is the fall.

It is further observed, and the honest man will admit, that each man will encounter within himself those weaknesses which he might have corrected sooner had he noted them, but he has instead discovered them through an unfortunate result. This is unavoidable and is a part of learning and being human, but pain may be minimized in frequency and severity by the application of deliberate and regular introspection.

Like any muscle, the mind atrophies without exercise. Sound thinking is not an accident, it is a decision. No one man is the fount of all knowledge and no one man always gets it right. As one may learn a thing by doing it, so too he may learn to reason by examining the process of his conscious, probative thoughts. One uncovers the diamonds by digging through the coal.

Critical thinking and wisdom are survival necessities in a world full of unscrupulous men who see a weak mind the way a hungry wolf sees a lamb. He who would be free must be able to think clearly; he must see through faulty reasoning and recognize false conclusions both in himself and in others. When it comes to training and utilizing one's critical faculties, the process of learning never ends and the need for the mind to be kept razor sharp is the cutting edge of eternal vigilance.

It is said that just as iron sharpens iron, so one person sharpens another.[7] We learn from each other; we learn from that brutal teacher - experience; we learn by sitting at the feet of those who have displayed mastery of a subject; we learn by observing, listening, reflecting and submitting to an absolute commitment to truth, wherever it may lead.

If we are not willing to think, we will never know true liberty, nor do we deserve it even though it is an integral part of our nature. Unfortunately it is also part of the nature of man to seek to gain advantage over other men who have not laid hold of their rightful prerogatives.

We have reached a critical place in the history of our nation. For over one hundred years, the wolves have been teaching men to be lambs and unless there is an awakening, the final slaughter of the lambs is imminent.

May this modest effort contribute to the alarm which is sounding throughout our land; wake up; get up; think; act!

2 - Is Freedom Really Fragile?

"America will never be destroyed from the outside. If we falter and lose our freedoms, it will be because we destroyed ourselves."
Abraham Lincoln

"If a nation expects to be ignorant and free, in a state of civilization, it expects what never was and never will be."
Thomas Jefferson to Charles Yancey in 1816

Freedom is both rare and fragile. That it should continue to bloom in our own country is a decision we must make as a people; we must choose to protect and defend freedom, and the Constitution that facilitates it, in the face of resolute, entrenched, and clever adversaries.

It is not the decision of a collective that is required. Collective decisions are for "sheeple" because they are usually made by someone else on our behalf, often against our will. It is a personal decision repeated by tens of millions of individuals throughout the land that will win the victory. One should not be deceived: if he is not standing on solid ground, he and his freedom will fall.

Furthermore, if one does not understand the nature of liberty; its inseparable union to responsibility and self control; its distinction from its counterfeit libertinism[8], he will be lured into a deception which is the plague of our modern culture; a culture of selfishness, victimhood, and entitlement that cannot coexist with true liberty.

One should not interpret this study as a rejection of the need for lawful government among men. We can and

Paul Phaneuf

do choose to exercise certain restraints and to adhere to common laws enacted by our representatives to facilitate and define the society in which we live. My argument is that our natural rights and the compact our forbears agreed to are meant to restrict the authority of government, not to constrain our personal options. This is a critical distinction. Upon whom were the chains of the Constitution placed? Not upon you and me as individuals, but upon the institution of government.

Most assuredly we are not to be ruled by our government, we are to be served by it. It is not the individual actions of honest free men that are limited by our Constitution; it is the government that is limited.

Let me rephrase this and say it again. It is the society we have formed and the government we have established that are governed. Except in very limited circumstances, government has no authority granted to it by the Constitution, or inherent in its being which invests it with the authority to rule over us. It is only by an illicit and unlawful use of force that government intrudes into our lives and attempts to harness us like horses so it can direct our movement and decisions.

Furthermore, society is governed for the benefit of people as individual human beings, not for the benefit of some superior collective as it may be defined by an elite group of "superior" beings telling us why we must obey arbitrary rules that have no purpose other than to control us.

The questions each of us must ask are critical in determining where we stand as individuals. It is not based on some silly notion of individual perfection. None of us is perfect. In this life, we never will be. Certainly the notion that our government is perfect is pathetic and laughable.

As is often true, the search for answers is rarely void of the anguish of soul searching, and the questioning of oneself and one's deep rooted prejudices and preconceptions.

Because how we think about these matters affects not only our present but the future of our children, we must embrace a process of self assessment and evaluation of circumstances that is the start of a life long journey. The questions are simple. The answers run deep and will be repeated and reframed throughout this book. The following questions will be examined more than once in these pages:

Who am I?

What do I believe?

Why do I believe it?

If one cannot determine the answer to these questions, he will bend every way the wind blows and in adversity he will break. Wisdom is acquired through experience grounded in truth.

Each of us must come to his own conclusions. He must think it through for himself. But please remember, the head is for thinking and the heart and emotions are for feeling and not the other way around. A man who acts after thinking but without feeling will too often be cold and lack compassion; a man who acts after feeling but without thinking is a mindless fool who will too often find himself the stooge of the former.

Let us begin with a simple question: is it realistic to believe that freedom, real liberty residing in and exercised by individuals, can function in a world so diverse? Is freedom just another word for chaos or is it actionable, genuine, and practicable?

Is Freedom Really Fragile?

freedom just another word for chaos or is it actionable, genuine, and practicable?

3 - Can We Be Free in an Imperfect World?

Neither the wisest constitution nor the wisest laws will secure the liberty and happiness of a people whose manners are universally corrupt.

Samuel Adams

"Freedom is not a gift bestowed upon us by other men, but a right that belongs to us by the laws of God and nature."

Benjamin Franklin

While we will be exploring the basis of how and what we think, along with the importance of firmly grasping principles that must be fully internalized to be equipped in an environment where controversy is inevitable and oppression the historical reality, it is important that we do so within a certain context.

Intricately woven into the fabric of sovereignty is its foundational ethos: Freedom. Furthermore, understanding freedom is necessary only in a social context. A lone man in the wild is always governed by the laws of nature, but he does not need to resolve conflicting issues regarding the nature of freedom in a society.

With that framework in mind, one must not fall victim to the ploy used by those who would discredit self government and its cousin free enterprise, because in its natural outworking by imperfect men it is found to be inconsistent. All systems are operated by imperfect men, therefore it would logically follow that all systems are necessarily inconsistent in practice and results.

Paul Phaneuf

The real question is which system produces the greatest good for the greatest number and is also compatible with the nature of man? That system is Liberty. Freedom works. There are those who would have us believe that it is quaint but outdated to believe in the "blessings of Liberty". They are our mortal enemies and are not satisfied with enslaving only us. They want our children too.

One must not be misled by charlatans and misanthropes who choose to project only the negative and focus on failures and shortcomings of the Founders' plans for limited government. These are the same people who have sabotaged this noble experiment for their personal benefit.

Part of the imperfection we must cope with in this world is the sad reality that there are people who have positioned themselves to gain fortune, power or prestige by enslaving other men. We are all familiar with the evils of overt slavery and are alert to avoid it, but the new slavery of this century is subtle and cleverly disguised. There are people for whom the coercive power of government is a useful tool. They particularly pollute our national government.

There is a notion that is so critical it will be repeated more than once in these pages. We have so long lived in a society where government has unlawfully inserted itself in our personal relationships and private affairs and contracts, it is difficult to imagine how many and varied institutions that would satisfy the needs of free people have been distorted or completely suppressed by the heavy hand of tyrannical government. Matters which we now routinely assume should be managed by bureaucrats would over time, in a truly free society, be handled by institutions, businesses, and charities that emerged in a culture of Liberty. The entangling weeds of government have choked out the normal, healthy response of free people meeting society's genuine needs.

So when we ask, "Does it really matter if we take the time to think these things through for ourselves?" the answer is a resounding yes! We may ask, "Aren't we already busy with surviving and trying to make it through each day?" The answer to that question is also yes, but like society, our personal actions and decisions have been distorted by the same heavy hand of out of control government and the perverted institutions that have grown in its anemic soil.

Yes, the world is imperfect, however, if we could remove the influence of men who are not merely imperfect but rather profoundly evil, those blessings of Liberty would be more than adequate to adapt to the challenges of our world. As we have already observed, all systems are implemented by imperfect men, and any system created by men will have its challenges. The Founders built their model of government knowing that there would be problems to overcome. History has shown that they were quite correct. But I for one would prefer to face life's challenges without the overseer's whip on my back, without the bureaucrats' army of enforcers waiting to confiscate and incarcerate me for daring to want the freedom God gave me.

Well, if evil men have been undercutting our Republic for many decades, one might understandably ask, "What's the big deal?

4 - What's the Big Deal?

"Freedom had been hunted round the globe; reason was considered as rebellion; and the slavery of fear had made men afraid to think. But such is the irresistible nature of truth, that all it asks, and all it wants, is the liberty of appearing."

Thomas Paine

We have come to the time when the weight of the ages has fallen upon us in a way our generation did not anticipate. In fact, many would argue, and perhaps you are among them, that we are rapidly approaching a catastrophic fall. We may be too late, but we pray that we are not. Less this sound like hyperbole, it is only we who are surprised.

We have been forewarned. The Founders feared this day, they warned against it, and they prescribed methods to avoid it knowing full well that history had confirmed a truth echoed by Ronald Reagan two hundred plus years later: that freedom was always only one generation away from extinction.

As I revised these remarks on September 11, 2012, eleven years after the horror of the attacks on the World Trade Center, the Pentagon, and the crash in Shanksville, Pennsylvania, and amid all the controversy that has since surrounded that fateful day, I conclude that the day of extinction of the fountain of liberty and that shining city on a hill is rapidly approaching unless we act to prevent it. On this same date, September 11, 2012 the United States lost an Ambassador and three other staffers in a diplomat-

Paul Phaneuf

ic outpost in Benghazi, Libya. As reports file in, it appears that they were deliberately abandoned; this is almost unspeakable. Perilous times are already upon us.

Most of us in the second half of the twentieth century, throughout the free world and certainly here in these United States of America, have lived in a protective mental bubble. We have grown up in a time of plenty and liberty that has been unknown to most of humanity. Admittedly it has not been any kind of utopian freedom among men. Such a time has never existed in man's recorded history so we are not guilty of some unique failure. Nevertheless, ours has been a season of unprecedented comfort for the masses of humanity when compared to any other civilization.

However, to our extreme detriment, we have slept while those who oppose liberty have corrupted our institutions. They have invaded our schools and poured lies and filth into the minds of our children, and have insidiously subverted our money and our government. They have done these things not because they are against freedom philosophically (they are not that intelligent), but rather because it obstructs their ravenous cravings for power or wealth.

Do not be deceived. It is not ambition that is the problem. No, the enemy is greed, not aspiration. To seek things higher, or better, or greater; to pursue excellence or worthy goals; to build an enterprise, or to aspire to success; these are not the enemy. This is a diversionary lie intended to belittle and thereby diminish the importance of Liberty in the hearts and minds of men.

The sentiment of aspiration, the desire to improve one's life is what fuels the engines of growth and the creation of wealth. This idea is developed further in the section later in this book entitled Free Enterprise or Socialism.

The man who wants to improve his own condition by taking what belongs to another diminishes himself as much as he diminishes the man from whom he would ask the government to steal. The society as a whole suffers because he who expects the government to take from another on his behalf has failed to add to the wealth of the whole by the contribution of his energy.

What greater force is there among men than the drive and enthusiasm of someone chasing a dream? Up early, sacrificing, working late, often for little immediate results; overcoming adversity, solving problems, charging through discouragement, often risking everything with no guarantees, and why? To build, to achieve, to create, to succeed; all of this is done by choice, of one's own free will, animated by authentic hope and a desire to win. This is free enterprise. This man does not take from anyone, but rather by his industry, he increases and contributes to all. It cannot happen except in a political environment that values freedom.

At this time, we must pose this question: what kind of warped sense of altruism would advocate taking from a hard working person who would be willing to risk everything, so that some public servant can justify stealing to give another's blood, sweat and tears to someone whom he has deemed worthy of the plunder? Have we not entrusted this public servant to lead in the protection and defense of our God-given, constitutionally protected property rights?

Advocates for redistribution euphemistically refer to this as "giving everybody a shot". In the socialist/progressive worldview the involuntary taking through the use of force from one hard working individual to give it to some other individual whom the redistributionist or others like him have selected is somehow praiseworthy. They insult our intelligence by calling this charity. It would appear that to the one who is doling out the stolen loot, there is some perverse satisfaction, some weird feeling that somehow they are "doing that which is good", as though one can be charitable with another person's belongings? We will look at this in greater depth, but to me, stealing is stealing.

It is as though booty that has been pillaged is some sort of vaccine against fear, or laziness, or complacency, or a lack of imagination, or industry, or effort. It inoculates the recipients so that they do not catch the disease of resourcefulness. That makes a certain sick kind of sense: those who would be overlords are not particularly enthused about "resourceful" underlings.

This kind of thinking offers a seductive but very perilous sedative in the light of the difficulties we all struggle with in life. We do not all have the opportunity to start from the same place. My father was industrious but he had only an eighth grade education. I had a friend who both his grandfather and father were successful industrialists. He learned things about success from them that my father could not teach me because he did not know them. Have I been somehow cheated by this circumstance of fate? Surely here life has cursed me and government should take from my friend and give some to me?

Take the comparison a little further. My father was a man of character but not of means. However, I knew I was loved by both my parents. Many are not. He who is loved has an advantage over he who is not, at least insofar as to the attainment of happiness. Am I to be punished because of the advantage I had of the blessing of a loving father and mother? Some people are raised by a single parent. Some are orphans.

Certainly I was greatly advantaged over those who were never loved. Am I indebted to those who were not loved? Have I deprived them of opportunity? Is there somehow less love available in the world because I was greatly loved by my parents?

In fact, isn't the opposite true? Despite the possibility that I may have exceeded the amount of love I might have been apportioned in the perfect world designed in the imagination of some government bureaucrat, there is actually more love in the world, not less. How can this be possible, when surely there is only so much love to go around?

Isn't it the responsibility of government to intervene and rectify this imbalance? Perhaps I should be beaten to compensate for my excess portion of love? Since we cannot possibly distribute evenly the excess love I greedily received, to "even the playing field" should the govern-ment at least require me to share in the misery of those who were loved less?

Take the matter further: some start with resources others lacked; family money or connections perhaps; maybe higher intellect or greater athletic ability; maybe even something as simple as better health. But don't we all deserve the same shot? Do you see the absurdity of such a thought process? It becomes justification for the intrusion of government know-it-alls in the name of attaining any conceivable utopian fantasy and "righting" any imagined "wrong".

And experience shows that where we start from is no guarantee of where we will end up. Helen Keller couldn't see, hear or speak but she went on through great adversity to international acclaim. Joni Eareckson Tada and Charles Krauthammer both overcame accidents that left them quadriplegics. Eareckson Tada became a respected author and motivational speaker, Krauthammer a respected author, Pulitzer Prize winner and commentator. There are limitless examples of people overcoming seemingly impossible odds to attain greatness from lowly or hugely disadvantaged beginnings.

What we have in common and ought to protect is the opportunity for everyone to move forward from where they are. That is the essence of equal opportunity: not that we start from the same place - a completely ridiculous notion dispelled by opening one's eyes; rather, it is that we all have the opportunity to create a new reality for ourselves regardless of our origins. The notion of equal opportunity is anathema to any but an environment of freedom, which is why it is so rare in the history of humanity.

If I am successful, my children and grandchildren may end up as one of those people who start out with better resources than with what I started (unless the government steals it first). It would seem that is up to me. It is not up to the government. Rationalizing stealing does not make for a better society. The saying is trite but true: the road to hell is paved with good intentions.

If one is in government and he really wants to give everyone "a shot", he must get his socialist obstructions out of everyone's way; get bureaucrats to find real jobs that create wealth, not just take other people's wealth; get revenue agents, banditos with badges, out of the confiscation industry; get radical environmentalists out of the regulation industry, and get what used to be red, white and blue and has become pink, yellow and green out of the way!

The insatiable beast we must castrate is the gluttonous craving to possess not just what one can produce or honestly acquire but rather the rapacious need to possess and control everything and its bastard child, the need to control everyone using the abusive, coercive powers of government.

It is the lust for what belongs to others, including their very capacity to pursue their own well being and destiny through creativity, risk, and industry. It is the pride of life, unrestrained by the urgency of conscience, engorging itself on whatever prey it chooses to hunt and devour. It is not money that has been said to be the root of all kinds of evil; it is the love of money.[9]

If we would be forthcoming, we acknowledge that while we have found ourselves immersed in abundance, there are those who could not or would not partake in the quest for a better life; some because they were content with less, some because they were lazy, and some because they lacked the ability, or were perhaps challenged by obstacles beyond their control.

For those who choose to be content with fewer material luxuries, let there be no judgment or shame. Clearly a successful life cannot be measured by things acquired. Many are those whose lives have manifested richness untouched by acquisitions. We admire those who have given their lives to the well being of others, to the outreach of consolation and comfort and genuine charity.

To those who settle for less because they choose not to chase for more, that too is their right. Who are we to judge?

To those whom life has dealt a disadvantaged hand, real freedom affords the opportunity for society to help through genuine, voluntary charity. Even in our current state where the true benefits of the abundance produced by a free society have been drastically impaired by tyranny with a happy face, institutions exist which model this type of giving.

Also, to our shame, the contamination of slavery which has polluted the entire human experience through all the pages of recorded history was all too recent even here on our continent, and its painful consequences linger still.

But only deluded hate mongers would deny that we have made substantial progress in overcoming those consequences, that the hearts of most earnest men have honestly confronted the evil spirits of bigotry within and sought to conquer their baser selves. In these past decades, in a spirit of forgiveness and reconciliation, we have many of us from every race and creed offered the hand of friendship to those who would accept it. Only the most contemptible among us have failed to extend it or declined to receive it.

No nation has done more for the cause of freedom among men than our own. Flawed as the experience has been, wealth, liberty, and charity have found succor in the bosom of a country founded on the values of the Judeo Christian culture and an acknowledgement that within the very fabric of creation, nature itself speaks to the existence of fundamental truths.

We may be confronted with the anomaly of the contradictions that tear at the hearts of men. Self interest and good intentions and the well being of society appear at times to be at odds. Yet, in the precepts of the values upon which the Founders built the edifice of government we find optimism. Why? Because we learn from the Judeo Christian perspective that birthed America's foundational hopes that our Creator is free and has made men in His image and likeness and that men mirror their Creator in that they yearn to breathe free. The American ideal speaks to self evident truths.[10]

Within this context, considering the responsibilities that are attendant to the liberties we have enjoyed, we have been taught and it may be independently reasoned and confirmed, the price of freedom is eternal vigilance. One may ask, however, vigilant how; of whom or what?

I would suggest that when the difficult times come, and they surely will, each man will have to be able to answer three questions to his own satisfaction in order to endure, and to perpetuate the essentials of our system of liberty.

From the lessons of history; from the pages of scripture; from one's deepest sensibilities and most rigorous reasoning and investigations; from the confirmation of undeniable evidence that satisfies his own soul, each individual who would become or remain free must know the answers, and be able to articulate fluently and accurately the same to others when called upon. So again let us ask,

Who am I?

What do I believe?

Why do I believe it?

5 - Can You Make Your Case?

"Rebellion to tyrants is obedience to God"

Benjamin Franklin

"A society that puts equality--in the sense of equality of out-come--ahead of freedom will end up with neither equality nor freedom. The use of force to achieve equality will destroy freedom, and the force, introduced for good purposes, will end up in the hands of people who use it to promote their own interests. On the other hand, a society that puts freedom first will, as a happy by-product, end up with both greater freedom and greater equality."

Milton Friedman (Free to Choose, 1980)

It is more than being able to "make your case" before another man. It is the foundation upon which one's convictions, his conscience and perhaps the sacrifice of his very life must rest. The man who must be convinced of what he believes and why he believes it is the man whose consciousness resides in his own body and mind. It is the soul of each individual, who feels and thinks and who seeks spiritual solace and the knowledge of truth, who must be satisfied.

When we face that moment of consequence, our response, our ability to endure and stay the course, to face whatever may be required of us, will depend upon the strength of our core beliefs. Emotional commitment and strength of will is not enough. Our heart, our reason, and our faith must be engaged or, in adversity, we will collapse under the weight of our fears and doubts. Or worse, we will succumb too soon to the scourge of the lash or incarceration that cruel and self righteous men would inflict on their fellow men because they could not bend their wills, or coerce them to worship at the altar of government.

My own convictions are based on my faith that the God of the Bible, while He has shown Himself to be necessarily just, He has shown Himself to be ultimately a God of mercy. History has demonstrated that the world, to the extent that it has suppressed liberty, is not merciful although there are impostors who would convince us that they themselves are otherwise.

Each man will answer the three questions that have been posed as he sees fit. However, regardless of one's personal beliefs, the greater portion of the western world at the time of the founding of our nation relied on the philosophical conclusions that flowed out of exposure to scripture for these answers. To deny this is to be blind to fact.

That those men were imperfect in their understanding and application of these scriptures is irrelevant. No man has ever perfectly applied any religious or philosophical system (except Jesus, say Christians). This is part of the challenge of how humanity has lived in fact. The Founders never sought a perfect union. They knew it was unattainable. They sought a "more perfect" union.[11]

Let me restate, my purpose is not to convince anyone of the truth of the Bible, but rather to examine how the western world centered its development on the principles and truths it espouses. It makes sense in a world going mad to know the source of the sanity in which it was once embedded. Thereby we might perhaps hope that we can again be grounded in those principles and once again inure to posterity freedom's proven advantages.

Is there a way to internalize and evaluate these truths for ourselves? Can truth be known at all? Does it even exist? How do we know what is the right course for ourselves, our families, our communities, our country?

6 - What Is Fairness?

"Human nature itself is evermore an advocate for liberty. There is also in human nature a resentment of injury, and indignation against wrong. A love of truth and a veneration of virtue. These amiable passions are the "latent spark"... If the people are capable of understanding, seeing and feeling the differences between true and false, right and wrong, virtue and vice, to what better principle can the friends of mankind apply than to the sense of this difference?"

John Adams

We live in world of experiences. Often they are hard and full of sorrow. They can sometimes be thrilling or maybe monotonous, at times magnificent, at other times grindingly difficult. They may occasionally be gentle and lovely, soft as a newborn, sweet as a lover's smile, even marvelous and intricate, perhaps delicate as spider's silk, and light as a whisper. We know a sunset can be inspiring, and that a sunrise wakes up the whole world around us. Sometimes life just feels good. And we know it when it does.

We accept that some things we cannot change. We deal with the pain, the loss that must come because life is short. We know that because we live, we must eventually die and for many years as we grow older we pretend that it cannot happen to us. But life catches up and we learn to take it as it comes, some of us better than others, but take it we must.

Yet through it all, within the deep that reaches outward from the heart of us, we sense intuitively that there is a right and a wrong. Call it right and wrong or good and evil; we know that it exists because we find it so readily in everyone around us, and in those honest moments, within ourselves. That person is unfair, we say; this one lies, and another is mean spirited. We even recognize the assault on some higher essence when we encounter someone who is arrogant. Who is he to put me down? Who is she to think she's better than the rest of us? Just who do they think they are?

We know. We know the jackboot reminds us of mindless hate. We know that stealing and murder are wrong. We know when something, some action is wrong when we see it, perhaps because it stirs an inner sense of outrage. And we know that we are seeing something very, very wrong in our country this very day. In our times, things are inside out and upside down. In a world of deception, the casualty is reality.

We know that the world is not fair, and we seem to sense it when some particular thing is unfair. We are quick to judge when someone commits an offense against us but we are slow to see the same fault in ourselves. This is not confined to one man but is common to all men. We deal daily with its effects and find that bailing water out of the leaky ship is a never ending necessity of life on the sea. It requires discipline. In life, we either discipline ourselves or we are disciplined by the inevitability of the law of consequences.

We are created free and we know we make mistakes. Because we find injustice and cruelty among men, we know we need a way to deal with these things in a manner that does not resort to anarchy or the injustice of the vigilante.

It is this desire to maintain peace that necessitates the formation of governments. Unfortunately the legitimization of coercion to maintain peace becomes the flame that attracts the moths of corruption. These immediately begin their infestation and attempts to turn the lawful and designated purpose of government into a tool to control others to benefit themselves.

And there are many things which we know but would prefer to ignore. There are unpleasant experiences, there is pain, there is poverty, there is injustice; but among the greatest sources of death and torment among men, there is tyranny. Dangerously, ironically, even in the act of warfare, in the guise of good intentions there is savagery and the abuse of power.

There is unease, a gnawing and agonizing tearing of the fabric of our inner peace, an unmistakable and deep sense of violation that disturbs the core of our deepest selves. It cannot be avoided except by a deliberate numbing of our powers of observation and a conscious effort to escape the revelations of self examination.

We are in a vortex and cannot escape the apprehension that all that we hold dear is plummeting into a sinkhole of confiscatory madness, a season of plunder, of benign pillaging, a tyranny disguised with a friendly smile.

This awareness brings us to the question each man must ask himself: if my observations about the state of this world are true, if the warning bells that clang incessantly in my psyche that tell me things are skewed are not mere madness, if my conscience and my reason speak truth to me, then what within me apprehends this violation?

If we are not among those who have chosen the sleep of fools, then what is it that speaks to us and warns us of impending catastrophe? That is a fair inquiry and is the question that we are pondering. It is my hope that within the thoughts we share one may find some answers worth considering. What is truth? Why do we even need to ask the question?

7 - What Is Truth?

Looking beyond the simplistic dictionary definitions, one observes that truth is the basis upon which all men may interact with confidence. It is the underlying source of trust in human relationships both personal and in commerce. Without it there can be no certainty, there can be no agreement, there can be no commitment, and there can be no peace.

These statements are substantiated by numerous maxims of law, truisms which are at the core of common law and the basis of our system of justice, at least before it was perverted by the ideology of redistribution and the progressive agenda which seeks to render us to the position of serfs.

Examples are:

Truth is the mother of justice.

Truth fears nothing but concealment.

He who does not willingly speak the truth is a betrayer of the truth.

The truth that is not sufficiently defended is frequently overpowered.

Paul Phaneuf

He who does not disapprove approves.

Silence is assent.

Herein lays a source of disagreement that has manifested among men of every era. The argument is framed thusly: there is no absolute truth. Truth is relative. What may be true for one, say some, may not be true for all.

They say truth, like the idea of God, is a victim of the great agnosticism: God is unknown or unknowable. The problem with this argument is that it flies in the face of science, reason, experience, and revelation. If truth be unknowable then life is unlivable.

Who would fly in a plane if the physics of aerodynamics could not be determined with certainty? While driving an automobile in America, why stay to the right if the rules of the road are in flux; after all, who can be certain that driving to the right is true to all men traveling the same road? Why look at a clock? What is 1PM to one may be 3AM to another, which is a drastic dilemma if they happen to live on the same street. If there is no truth, there can be no reality.

The entire basis of the insurance industry is based on the assumption that life as a whole is actuarially predictable. It is a utilitarian convenience of miscreants and tyrants to claim that truth does not exist, that it is only an illusion.

Truth forces accountability and that restrains the actions of men. And that is the heart of the matter. There are only three types of people who claim that truth does not exist, who deny that it has a reality independent of whether or not people perceive it: the misinformed, the dishonest, and the insane. Anyone who has interacted with any one of the three knows the grief that these types of individuals cause to their fellow men.

If we are to live in harmony with our fellow human beings, we must acknowledge that truth is, otherwise we can know nothing. Is not life sufficiently difficult because we do not know enough? Do we have to make it impossible by declaring that we can know nothing?

But where do we start? How can we know?

8 - What Are We Searching For?

"How strangely will the Tools of a Tyrant pervert the plain Meaning of Words!"
Samuel Adams

"As each situation in life represents a challenge to man and presents a problem for him to solve, the question of the meaning of life may actually be reversed. Ultimately, man should not ask what the meaning of his life is, but rather he must recognize that it is he who is asked. In a word, each man is questioned by life; and he can only answer to life by answering for his own life; to life he can only respond by being responsible."
Viktor E. Frankl, **MAN'S SEARCH FOR MEANING**

The Declaration of Independence states that each man is endowed by his Creator with certain unalienable rights. This foundational assertion inevitably brings us to the notion of God. In one form or another we all deal with the issue of God. As a young man searching to understand the paradoxes and inconsistencies in human behavior, including my own, I considered myself a seeker. We all want answers.

Like many of you, I was brought up in the religion of my parents. As I got older I lost interest and began to look elsewhere because I could not find answers to questions about life that many people struggle with. Why do good things happen to bad people? Why do bad things happen to good people? Does God even care? Do gods even exist? These are almost universal questions which are hardly unique to me. However, finding answers is a struggle many people prefer not to deal with.

Paul Phaneuf

I was about nine years old when I started struggling to make sense of what I was being taught; but in my early twenties, a precipitating event was the death of my mother. She died young and unexpectedly. I began my search for truth and the meaning of life in earnest. I had to know. What happened to her? Was it possible she might be happy, or worse unhappy, or was she just gone? I did not trust the beliefs I held at the time.

I studied and read mystics, Eastern sages, and the great books of other religions. I read the Tao, the Dhammapada, the Upanishads, and the Baghavad Gita.

I read books by hippies, mystics, doctors, and New Age gurus who entertained concepts from all over the spectrum; from the efficacy of drugs, the powers of the creative mind, the rejection of rationality, even the denial of existence. I read pop titles like ZEN AND THE ART OF MOTORCYCLE MAINTENANCE (just in case), BE HERE NOW, AUTOBIOGRAPHY OF A YOGI. The list goes on and on. I'm unable to remember all the authors and titles but there were hundreds over the years. I read incessantly.

My purpose in sharing these thoughts is not to impugn what others may have found to be sufficient for them, but rather to emphasize that my quest was not taken casually. It seemed to me logical that truth was discoverable. Was my hope that somewhere, somehow, someone would bring me to an answer that would explain the relationship between the natural and the supernatural unrealistic? Why couldn't an explanation exist that would make sense to a real person in the real world, me?

Nothing that I read helped me to take my observations about life and link them satisfactorily to some supernatural explanation. Nothing that was supposed to be "out there" helped me to understand what the world appeared to be right here. Where were the real answers? Anyone who has wandered in the land of the philosophical and spiritual unknown can confirm the length and breadth of that internal landscape. In retrospect, more than once I could not or did not find the "exit" sign out of spiritual wastelands quickly enough.

At that stage of my life I rejected the Bible and did not read it because the whole notion of God becoming a man and dying on a cross was ridiculous to me.

I read from the Quran, but I could not reconcile acknowledging Jesus as a great prophet while simultaneously calling him a liar, and that is what the Quran seemed to be saying to me. Although at the time I could not have cared less about Jesus, I did care about consistency and could not get past what seemed to me a self contradictory position, so to continue there was to my mind a waste of time. [See this endnote for a warning about radical Islam:[12]]

Finding no satisfactory answers to my questions, I eventually shook my fist at God and declared that if He had expectations of me that it was His responsibility to communicate them to me or He was not much of a God. God was probably not impressed with my tantrum. However, after much internal turmoil, I eventually came to a very personal conclusion: if God exists, if He has standards to which He will hold me accountable, if there really is a God, then He[13] surely has to have communicated His expectations in no uncertain terms and in a venue that ought to be discernible.

After years of resisting and contrary to my preference that God should conform to my standards (frankly, that he should be kind of like an obedient puppy), I reluctantly accepted that God to be God could not be a product of my imagination. God did not work if I created Him. At first, that was a disappointment. As much as I hated to admit it - and I will explain later how it came about - but when I eventually read the Bible, I realized that God had to be a cause and not an effect.

For me it was not easy. After much study, I had tried with all my might to find any reasonable explanation other than Christianity (as I have admitted, I did not want to believe "that stuff"), I came to the conclusion that the Bible is the communication to men that I had concluded it was God's responsibility to provide. It had been in front of my face all along. Truth may be hidden by others, or we may choose to look away, but it does not hide itself. Truth is not always convenient, but it is persistent and eventually unavoidable.

Now if you are not a Christian or a Jew you have every right to ask why you should care the slightest about my little story. It is a reasonable response and here is why I shared it. Take my name and story out and put yours in. We all have one when it comes to spirituality, and particularly with what we call religion.

Here is what is compelling: we are not unique when it comes to this angst of the soul. There is universality about the experience of some sort of spiritual quest that runs through the entire history of humanity. From ancestor worship, to worshiping the stars, to gods that demanded human sacrifice, humans have sought to fill an inner vacuum with some responsive spirit that would speak to us because we sense something within us that listens.

The alternative is to believe that all is nothing. Everything is nothing. Everyone is nothing. Life is meaningless. It is all an accident. Had I ever met anyone in life or in the books I read who thought in that way and nevertheless lived a joyful life, my search for truth and meaning would have ended there. I never did. In fact, I have found the opposite. The louder one objects to the call of a God in the life of others (let alone his own), the angrier that person seems to be. Are there any truly happy atheists?

Now many of those who like to pretend that truth is some kind of fable also like to claim that they are above faith. Faith is for the gullible. What does that really mean and is it even possible to live without faith?

9 - Is Any Man Without Faith?

"Now faith is being sure of what we hope for and certain of what we do not see."

Hebrews 11:1 (NIV)

One may have met some men, or read the works of other men who professed to be atheists, but no man can claim convincingly that he has no faith. The definition of faith given by the writer of Hebrews says nothing about God or religion. It speaks to the very heart of what faith is. As a point of comparison, let us consider it by looking at how it has evolved in my own life. Any can take out my details and substitute them with his own.

Because we all die, in the end no one can claim to have personal experience of what happens when a man reaches the point of no return. It does not matter what one believes about what happens after death; whatever it is that he believes and trusts about what can never be scientifically verified is a matter of faith.

If one accepts or denies an afterlife, he is making a statement that he is sure of what he hopes for. He either hopes that when this mortal life ends, there is nothing; or he hopes there is reincarnation or some other possibility. If one is not a Christian he certainly is hoping that Christians are wrong. Regardless, he and I are both saying that we are certain of what we do not see.

Not to disparage the experiences of those who may or may not have experienced a type of death and nevertheless

Paul Phaneuf

found themselves back in their bodies, everyone acknowledges that there is a certain death from which there is no coming back. How can anyone pretend that every person is a not person of faith when no living man can see beyond the grave?

The point is that it cannot be contradicted that everyone reaches the conclusion where death is the end of all that we may know on this side of eternity. At that point, as it pertains to what comes afterwards, regardless of what one believes does one not operate in faith?

In the end, some have found the object of their faith to be wanting and fragile. Despite lives lived vociferously mocking the God of Christianity, Nietzsche died insane and incoherent; Voltaire was a Deist and is said to have cried out with his dying breath, "I am abandoned by God and man, I shall go to hell." But even they lived and died believing in "something".

Although never an atheist, competing ideas offered at best an agnostic "faith" that battled within me and yielded only the sense that God was unknown or unknowable. That kind of faith was no more satisfying for me than it seems to have been for Nietzsche or Voltaire. Mine was a conscious albeit frustrating search for "truth". As indicated earlier, the experience that compelled me to search for some kind of certainty about the nature of life was the death of my mother in her forties. Despite my religious upbringing, to my mind the ultimate question remained unanswered: what happens when you die? What, if anything, was the state of being of my mother?

Although the object of the faith to which my doubts have since surrendered has proven itself to be sufficient for others in even the most horrific of circumstances, it is nevertheless still faith. Faith is not foolish, nor is it futile to want to understand it. It is hard to imagine living life without faith as one of the consciousness tools that we utilize to deal with even the routine aspects of life.

The following details of my personal journey are offered to illustrate that identifying the source of one's own faith is an unavoidable process for any rational being. Your own experience may be similar, or not, or perhaps you have not yet decided that this is a necessary exercise for you. However, it is a rewarding and important journey we each must take if we are to know how our own mind comprehends, and why we believe whatever it is that we believe.

In my case, the catalyst was a long conversation with my brother. He had been a Christian for many years, and it was after one of our many talks during which I told my brother (again) that I could not "buy into" Christianity. However, I promised that I would at least give the Bible a read. I had never bothered. While I thought Christianity was foolish, I did not think my brother a fool. So I thought *I'm not afraid of a book. I've read thousands of them, why not the Bible?* It seemed to be a risk free concession. I had rejected his Christian beliefs, but after all, it was just a book. It wouldn't be the first useless book I had ever read.

In the reading of it, to my surprise, it spoke to me. In its message, God whispered directly to me. One may dismiss it if he chooses, and I understand why he might, but that was my experience.

Now whatever he believes, surely the following fact must give one pause to reflect: this encounter with some otherness that claims to be God, and speaks to men through the pages of scripture has been the shared experience of many witnesses through all of Western Civilization (and throughout the world).

The Old Testament offered a covenant between men and God in writings that have come down through the ages for over four thousand years.

The New Testament has told the story of Jesus and taught His doctrines for over two thousand years. The Bible was not written twenty years ago. One may reject its theology but to deny its impact on our culture and its longevity denies the obvious and is not intellectually honest. Books are written and quickly forgotten when people do not find any value in them. Something has sustained the faith of so many for so long. What could it be?

10 - Faith in What?

"The general principles, on which the Fathers achieved independence, were the only Principles in which that beautiful Assembly of young Gentlemen could Unite, and these Principles only could be intended by them in their address, or by me in my answer. And what were these general Principles? I answer, the general Principles of Christianity, in which all these Sects were United: And the general Principles of English and American Liberty, in which all those young Men United, and which had United all Parties in America, in Majorities sufficient to assert and maintain her Independence.

"Now I will avow, that I then believe, and now believe, that those general Principles of Christianity, are as eternal and immutable, as the Existence and Attributes of God; and that those Principles of Liberty, are as unalterable as human Nature and our terrestrial, mundane System."

John Adams

Now this attention to faith and how it affects our thinking is relevant to the kind of country we have become. We find that in today's America that the actions of our government are in conflict with its obligations to our individual sovereignty. We observe a willingness to deny what is obvious every day among men to whom we have entrusted power and it usually makes us furious because it occurs in the most implausible situations imaginable. The excuses given by those we have elected to serve us as a reason to compromise our liberty are innumerable.

Inexplicably many of us have placed our faith in an institution that is itself mindless, that has been taken over by individuals who are deceitful, and who treat us like we are

Paul Phaneuf

stupid. By trusting government we almost deserve their contempt, because we have for so long chosen not to oppose brazen behavior that should nullify the faith we have placed in it.

It is not that we cannot identify this contradictory behavior in ourselves and others when we see it, but sometimes we do not take note of what we see because of the nature of the world we live in. Compared to the crying baby, the requirements of our obligations, or the bills coming due at the beginning of the month, concern about the object of our faith does not draw our attention because it does not seem imminent compared to life's daily challenges.

But ignoring the obvious, which often times is as simple as common sense, permeates the core of our government to our detriment. It seems to be an operational imperative of all three branches of the federal government. How else could they take the plain meaning of the Constitution and act in a manner that any fool can see is contrary to its enumerated powers and the Founders' deliberate intent to constrain those powers?

Our public servants' blindness to the obvious, whether intentional or not, is destructive to our freedom and the fabric of our society. It renders free markets inoperable. It perverts judgment and makes reasonable cooperation impossible; it is at the heart of our frustration, and aggravates our national malaise and decay. This is the consequence of living in a culture of deception that bombards our senses continuously.

What we are saying here is that our detachment from the need to address what faith means to us is a picture of how little we pay attention to what freedom means to us. We all suffer the consequences for this dysfunctional mindset, and that is why we must, and even need to address it. That is why this discussion about the nature of faith is relevant even though it may seem unimportant and hides in the raucous noise of life. After all, a fish does not pay attention to water until there is none.

Have you had some defining experience that identified and confirmed what it is that you place your faith in? Regardless of what its object may be, can you agree that every man has faith in something, even if it is faith exclusively in his own thinking?

This is important. The difference among us is the object of our faith. This is for some an uncomfortable reality and is difficult to swallow and digest. Are you one of those who have placed your faith in government? It is not an inconsequential consideration. Have you identified what is the object of your own faith?

The Founders surely did. It is fair to ask, is there any justification for the Founders' reliance on the principles that the Bible teaches? Can any rational standards be applied to shed light on that question?

11 - So Who Says What's True?

*"Of all the dispositions and habits, which lead to political pros-
perity, Religion and Morality are indispensable supports. In vain
would that man claim the tribute of Patriotism, who should labor to
subvert these great pillars of human happiness, these firmest props of
the duties of Men and Citizens. The mere Politician, equally with the
pious man, ought to respect and to cherish them. A volume could not
trace all their connexions with private and public felicity. Let it
simply be asked; where is the security for property, for reputation, for
life, if the sense of religious obligation desert the oaths, which are the
instruments of investigation in Courts of Justice? And let us with
caution indulge the supposition, that morality can be maintained
without religion. Whatever may be conceded to the influence of refined
education on minds of peculiar structure, reason and experience both
forbid us to expect, that national morality can prevail in exclusion of
religious principle."*

George Washington

Returning to our former point, interestingly, the Bible is the only book that claims within its pages to be the very word of God. Many books claim to speak to spiritual matters, or to have revelatory authority from some angelic being, but only the Bible declares repeatedly that it is God speaking. It is understandable that many find this implausible, but at least one may admit that it is interesting. If true it is profound; if false, it is deplorable. The Founders for the most part believed it to be true.

One translation, the King James Bible, says "thus saith the Lord" 430 times in the Old Testament. Over 48 times the Bible refers to itself as the "word of God". Imagine once more the contemptible hubris of such a claim if it is false. Such a claim, if false, is beyond despicable; it is manic.

Yet we find that for these thousands of years men have heard or read, and astonishingly, believed these claims. Many died martyrs' deaths believing the words to be true. Consider the utter stupidity of the human race if it could not recognize abject nonsense in the practical outworking of their day to day lives over a span of millennia. Surely even advocates of atheistic evolution would render some significance to this fact?

It is one thing to have lived in a time of scientific error; it may be wrong about the moon being made out of cheese, but it is an entirely different matter to starve to death waiting for it to fall out of the sky onto a plate. The first is a silly notion; the second is the mark of an imbecile. Could billions of people over thousands of years have all been pathetic fools?

What possible condition could have contributed to this longevity except that the truths espoused by the Bible ordered men's lives and comforted their souls? It is beyond comprehension that delusion has been the hallmark of what men have felt in their hearts regarding their relationship with God through Scripture for thousands of years.

At some point, despite our personal misgivings we must give some kind of credence to an experience among our fellow men that appears nearly universal. Many would be fearful to have surgery without anesthesia, yet in China this is done all the time using acupuncture. Are millions of Chinese pretending that surgery under acupuncture is painless?

Rather I must conclude that I am not fully informed. In fact, after reading the Bible, that is what I concluded, at least eventually. But that was my experience. If the substance of what you believe is not the same as mine, have you at least questioned and sought to comprehend the transcendental depths of your own mind and spirit?

Allow me to state the obvious. There is significance in the fact that the confirmation that men have received regarding the Bible's impact upon them was based not only on what they believed, but also on what they experienced. That one man might claim to hear an inner voice can generally not be confirmed. That billions of men should hear the same voice over thousands of years is astonishing and cannot be reasonably dismissed. It would be a challenge to argue that such an event is not significant.

Many men refuse to even read the Bible. I was one of them. Within the framework of our consideration of the source and authority of truth there is significance to the fact that through the tides of history men have managed to preserve this book through persecution, conquest, controversy, banning, and untold numbers of attempts at eliminating its existence. Somehow the human race has chosen to defend it against the onslaught of empires, despots, and tyrants (or as believers would declare, God has preserved it). A needful question must be asked: why?

Certainly the Founders asked these kinds of questions. And most assuredly not all of them were Christians. Jefferson created his own set of scriptures and cut out all the references to the miracles of Jesus. But he constantly affirmed the principles which the scriptures espoused and he called himself a believer in the doctrines that Jesus taught.

It is this kind of question that every man must answer if he wants to live free in a world that challenges everything in the name of anything. We may arrive at different conclusions about miracles than Jefferson, but one must respect that he thought it through to his own satisfaction. The point is, he thought. He reflected. He used his mind. He sought to understand what he believed.

Why did men like the Founders confirm the efficacy of scriptures as the basis for a civilized society and a structure for self government? The answer is because within its pages, the human race has found principles and guidance that have stood the test of time, reason, and conscience. There are some things which speak to our inner spirit and declare themselves to be valid. To deny them wrenches our souls. The Laws and God of the Bible have spoken to the needs of men. As Francis Schaeffer put it, God is there and He is not silent.[14]

The intent here is not to persuade anyone that the Bible is the Word of God. It is not a theological point that we are considering. That is far and away not even remotely possible in these few pages. The beauty of our way of life, of our Constitutional Republic, of the First Amendment, is that every man is free to believe or not to believe as he sees fit.

What cannot be denied is that the Founders believed that freedom is itself a gift from God and they enshrined that belief in our Founding documents. History is clear. The principles the Bible espouses and the Laws it declares have served as the bedrock of Western Civilization for centuries.

Here is an important point: authentic principles are valid regardless of their source, meaning that if they are based on Judeo Christian precepts, they are impactful whether one is, or is not, a Christian or a Jew. One need not be Christian or Jewish to be influenced by the Judeo Christian ethic, which is the bedrock of our civilization and the Founders' ethos. The question becomes, is there any consequential significance to this statement if true?

12 - Did The Founders Believe The Bible?

"The right to freedom being the gift of God Almighty, it is not in the power of man to alienate this gift and voluntarily become a slave... These may be best understood by reading and carefully studying the institutes of the great Law Giver and Head of the Christian Church, which are to be found clearly written and promulgated in the New Testament."

Samuel Adams

An honest examination of the original writings of the Founding Fathers of these United States of America shows that the overwhelming majority of them were clearly devout Christians and their lives and thoughts centered on its teachings.

One need only to read what they wrote and two things are a given. They wanted a country where people of any religion could practice freely. They believed that the values of the Christian faith were essential to the survival of Liberty.

To them, the moral principles, the personal freedom, the individual responsibility, and the submission to an authority other than man himself are demanded by the Bible. They were convinced this was absolutely crucial to the success of their noble experiment with self government.

They knew that self government depends on self restraint, that freedom without responsibility degenerates into wanton licentiousness and profane self indulgence, and that ultimately this would destroy the Republic. We are watching these consequences play out before our very eyes.

Paul Phaneuf

The Founders held some truths to be "self-evident". They did not debate these matters. Certain truths were above the discriminatory faculties of men. For the Founders it was self evident that the intricacy and expanse of the heavens pointed to a Creator.[15] They believed that Nature itself spoke to the existence of a God. The Declaration of Independence speaks to the Laws of Nature and Nature's God.

It is these very observations that led the Apostle Paul to declare that the unseen things that God has made are clearly visible and that they demonstrate and display his power and divinity, so much so, that men have no excuse for denying his existence.[16]

This reference is not to proselytize but to demonstrate what the world has found in Scripture: the authority of truth confirmed in daily life.

If you do not believe these things to be true, and hopefully a sufficient number of you who do not so believe have nevertheless continued to this point, then the question remains: have you examined what it is that you do believe? Can you answer this to your own satisfaction? Not to mine. I am irrelevant; but to your own satisfaction?

Have you concluded that you observe a hierarchy in nature- insentient beings (plants), creatures that are alive but function only on a preprogrammed level (ants, bees); higher levels of creatures like mice and squirrels; animals that seem to interact with humans like horses and dogs; and creatures that think, reflect, create, communicate complex ideas, like us? Can we learn anything about life from these observations?

13 - What Is Your Place?

"The fundamental source of all your errors, sophisms and false reasonings is a total ignorance of the natural rights of mankind. Were you once to become acquainted with these, you could never entertain a thought, that all men are not, by nature, entitled to a parity of privileges. You would be convinced, that natural liberty is a gift of the beneficent Creator to the whole human race, and that civil liberty is founded in that; and cannot be wrested from any people, without the most manifest violation of justice."

Alexander Hamilton

Regardless of one's personal spiritual faith or presumed lack thereof, no honest broker of facts and ideas can deny that our country was founded upon readily discernible principles. One does not need to be a physicist to acknowledge gravity.

While this may annoy some (we Christians after all can be a persistent lot), no authentic thinker can deny that the freedom to express one's conscience in matters of faith is a fundamental aspect of the Christian tradition. With all due respect to those who would find this discussion to be a sneak attack by Christians who want to convert the world and install a theocracy, our claim simply acknowledges the basic truths that underpinned America's moral and political paradigm at the time of its founding.

It is a core belief among Biblical scholars that the God of the Bible has always given men the freedom to accept or reject His Lordship. In both the Old and New Testaments, God makes His will known to men, but as indicated earlier in this work, according to the scriptures He has fashioned them "in His image and likeness."[17] He created man free. This speaks to the concept of man as a sovereign being under God and therein is its relevance. There is no being that is freer than God and there are no creatures more free than those whom such a God has created and set free.

There is a maxim of law which states that "The power which is derived cannot be greater than that from which it is derived." Simply put this means that the man cannot be greater than the God who created him.

Following that line of thought, is it not logical that the State cannot be greater than the men who created it? The federal government cannot be greater than the sovereign colonial states that sent those free men that created it. Who can deny that today this logical order has been reversed? We live in a political delusion where the tail is wagging the dog. The federal government has placed itself at the top of the power pyramid and has essentially placed itself above the States, Man, and God.

Do you believe the government to be superior to you? In the hierarchy of things, when it comes to government, are you the bug or the rat or the dog? What is your place?

14 - What Is The God Of Our Age?

"Society in every state is a blessing, but government, even in its best state, is but a necessary evil; in its worst state an intolerable one; for when we suffer or are exposed to the same miseries by a government, which we might expect in a country without government, our calamity is heightened by reflecting that we furnish the means by which we suffer."

Thomas Paine

"When men enter into society, it is by voluntary consent; and they have a right to demand and insist upon the performance of such conditions and previous limitations as form an equitable original compact."

Samuel Adams

The federal government demands obedience and reverence that is due only to the Supreme Being. This is a deep perversion of the commands of God. The State today demands tribute far beyond its lawful and Constitutional requirements. The State now demands the sacrifice of our blood, sweat, and tears. It demands of us, contrary to Biblical law, what only God may require. In the Bible, God has said that He alone is God and we are to have no gods before Him.[18]

The government of these United States of America has subverted the very essence of the men and women who are created in God's image. It is government that has become the greatest violator of the Law, and the first Law that government breaks is the Law that restricts it in how it

Paul Phaneuf

impacts the sovereign States and the Sovereign Men who created it.

The Founders considered government to be a monster, a necessary evil that needed to be contained, chained as they put it. They knew that history had shown them that the power afforded government is a seductive temptress and it calls not only to those who are willing to serve but also to those who would abuse it for their own purposes. This force has for most of human history been in the hands of the few and has been used to suit their purposes. Abusers of the people have always used the pretext of trashing them for their own good.

Today our government is largely in the clutches of forces that are hostile to Liberty. We must recognize that government has become antagonistic to the foundational beliefs from which the justification of Liberty is derived. It is itself a beast which has escaped the cage in which it was placed and now seeks to enslave the masters who contained it.

But creatures formed in the likeness of an infinitely free Being must have freedom as a component element of their nature. One can no more remove freedom from the inherent makeup of a man than one can remove his mind or his lungs without destroying not just who he is but what he is. From this self evident truth flows the life stream of the quality of being human.

Men owe their primary allegiance to God and not to government. Our government now demands that "We the People" should bow at the altar of temporal power. This, men of conscience who rely on Biblical Law and precepts, cannot do.

Men who seek to justify the absolute nature of government power love to abuse Jesus' answer to the Priests, who sought to trick him into apparent rebellion to Roman rule. When asked if men should pay taxes to their Roman masters, Jesus asked whose portrait was on the coin. They said Caesar's and Jesus responded, "Render to Caesar the things that are Caesar's and to God the things that are God's."[19] Coincidentally, this was Hitler's favorite Bible verse. Jesus tripped them by asking a question and giving an answer that to my mind gave them nothing. The fact is all things belong to God.[20]

Caesar, even as a tyrannical dictator was there only because God allowed it. Caesar was a pauper and a vassal subject to God. Our federal government is a servant. The obligation of loyalty to which we owe government stems not from its own nature but from the nature of God and our obligations to Him.

Love of country and love of government are not the same. Love is not something we feel for our government unconditionally, and obviously not if a government hostile to Liberty has morphed the nation into some kind of aggressive alien species which is out to devour us. I love America. As the song says, this land is your land; this land is my land. Love of country and loathing of tyrannical government are not antagonistic feelings. They are complementary.

Frankly, hating tyranny is effortless. Any anger will do. Liberty requires effort. It must be known, cherished, nurtured, defended and taught. It is living in a country that does these things that makes it worth loving.

Patriotism is similar, but not identical. It is something we owe each other because of our mutual commitment. I am a Patriot, but I can only pledge fidelity to the nation if it conforms to the terms of the founding compacts, and which the government is supposed to serve as dictated by the Constitution; and even then - only if it also conforms to the Laws of Nature and Nature's God. The government has forgotten its place, but I have not. We cannot.

If our country is represented by red, white and blue, I have pledged to honor red, white and blue. If self-serving cabals execute a bloodless coop over time, if it becomes apparent that the country is now pink, yellow and green, I do not care what statutes their droids pass that demand that I salute pink, yellow and green; I will not do it. I think. I must answer to my own conscience.

I will verify my conclusions against the authority of Scripture and against the documents to which we have mutually pledged our support. I do not believe that I have the right to arbitrarily pick and choose on the basis of what suits my whimsy. I will listen in good faith to honorable men who advise that I must reconsider, that I am mistaken; but if large numbers of the population are crying out with me, "The Emperor has no clothes!" I will not applaud his nakedness and bow in blind obedience.

Our flag and the pledge of allegiance are symbolic of these understandings.

We pledge allegiance "to the flag of the United states of America and to the Republic for which it stands...

[key words not to be taken lightly — I owe no allegiance to that which morphs out of the perversion of what it is supposed to stand for],

...One Nation, under God

[And all that this implies and construes],

...indivisible, with liberty

[And all that this implies and construes],

...and justice

[And all that this implies and construes]

...for all."[21]

Patriotism is a lovely and honorable sentiment if properly understood, but blind patriotism, my government, right or wrong patriotism is the tool of tyrants.

Hitler's Germany was the Fatherland. Stalin's Russia was the Motherland. This mindset makes all inhabitants the children of the government. "Mommy-land" and "Daddy-land" start as the benevolent nanny state and ends as the abusive parents, drunk on unrestrained power, entitled to dictate to and discipline unruly, disruptive, stupid children.

America is the land of the free and the home of the brave. Our government is the child of our dreams for freedom and is only legitimate and lawful when it remains limited, chained as the Founders intended. It was not constructed to "lord it over us." When our government at any level steps outside the box, it is the government that is the unruly child needing correction and restraining.

America is a way of life that must be lived out. It is nothing more than empty words if we are to render it blind allegiance. America is the blood, sweat, and tears of those who went before us and secured and protected Liberty on our behalf; it is our blood, sweat, and tears as we live the dream of Liberty, and when necessary, fight and die for it, mixing our blood, sweat, and tears with those who preceded us for the sake of those loved ones we may leave behind and the children who are yet to come, just as the Founders did.

It is a subservient government that we pledge allegiance to; one that serves, preserves the peace, provides for the common defense, and promotes the common good by securing the blessings of Liberty. Anything else is an impostor, and we owe no loyalty to interlopers, or frauds, or counterfeits.

Our government is structured in layers, each of which has a primary duty to the requirements of the Laws of Nature and Nature's God and the unalienable rights granted by our Creator.

Local government serves the needs of local free individuals and is itself subject to the restrictions of natural law.

The State government serves free men, overseeing local government, but not inherently superior to it; in fact subservient to it as it is further removed from the sovereign man than local government.

The federal government is the creation of free men through their servant State governments. It is subject to Natural Law and limited by the Constitution, inferior to the States and sovereign men and women. The federal government has been granted enumerated powers by the people, through the States, via the political compact that is the original Constitution agreed to in 1789.

As originally constructed it was constrained by the Ambassadorial function of Senators who prior to the 17th amendment saw their primary responsibility as protecting the sovereignty of their individual States. The federal government has zero lawful authority to interfere in the honorable, voluntary, and self-willed activities of men made free by their Creator.

The Courts, in whatever guise and at whatever level, have the responsibility of administering true Law, arbitrating the honest contracts entered into voluntarily by free men, and interpreting all statutes, treaties, regulations and rules through the prism of individual liberty and the constraints of the Supreme Law of the Land.

Liberty is the first filter through which any action of government must be measured. It is the finest filter of all with the tiniest mesh and most actions of governments do not lawfully pass through that barrier; but "We the People" have lowered our standards and submitted to the boot on our neck because our neighbor's foot is in it. Stupid, blind trust contrary to the laws of nature yields bondage and habitual tolerance of oppression, and invites the constrictions of incremental, cleverly camouflaged slavery.

We Love our country because of what it represents, not because its servant government has inherent worth in and of itself. Government is a construct of free men. It is not an entity that sits on Mount Olympus. It is a servant tool. It is subordinate, not superior. We do not bow before any throne except the throne of God. Our forefathers risked their lives and limbs to purchase that opportunity for themselves and their posterity. It is a possession each of us must individually lay claim to. They did so that we might live out our lives in the liberty that was God's grant and gift to every man. Only bonded fools forget these truths.

Our Founders believed that our nation had a manifest destiny, but it was not because it was a special piece of land or geographic or political entity, although God did in fact "shed his grace" on us in those regards.

To them it represented a mutual commitment, an ideal in the hearts of men. It represented their hopes to live out their lives according to the Laws of Nature and Nature's God. They established a government that recognized that men were endowed by their Creator with certain unalienable rights; they pledged their lives, their fortunes, and their sacred honor so that we, and they, and theirs would be secure in life, liberty and the pursuit of happiness.

They were resolved that they would be neither molested nor infringed upon by that which was a lower order (government) to the detriment of a higher order (man) that owed its Liberty to the highest order (God). To this I pledge my allegiance and to nothing less.

If the Founders did not trust government, however carefully constructed, and warned repeatedly of its unceasing threat, should we not do likewise?

15 - Does Power Really Corrupt?

"If ye love wealth better than liberty, the tranquility of servitude better than the animating contest of freedom, go home from us in peace. We ask not your counsels or your arms. Crouch down and lick the hands which feed you. May your chains set lightly upon you, and may posterity forget that ye were our countrymen."

Samuel Adams

"We, the people are the rightful masters of both Congress and the courts, not to overthrow the Constitution, but to overthrow men who pervert the Constitution."

Abraham Lincoln

The history of humankind has been marked by cruelty, bloodshed, slavery, misery, hunger, and tyranny. In the twentieth century alone, more people were murdered by their own governments' tyrannical policies than by all the wars and civil wars in that century combined.[22] One should reflect on the implications of that for a moment, especially if he is inclined to blindly entrust his freedom to the instrument of government.

This fact is so consequential that it bears repeating. It is so incredulous that we are inclined to dismiss it as just another exaggeration, but it is a hard numerical reality. More people were murdered in the twentieth century by governments' brutal actions against their own people than by all the wars and civil wars combined. This is monumentally shocking and sobering. This carnage is not new to human history.

Paul Phaneuf

It is common knowledge that the Founders of this nation were learned men who were acutely aware of their unique mission and destiny. It is a documented fact that the Founders were conscious of the pernicious and self serving actions of governments and those who would use its coercive powers to serve their own ends.

Through all of recorded history, only one nation has ever acknowledged that its existence was dependent upon the consent of the governed, that its power emanated from the people by virtue of the nature imparted to them by their Creator, that the existence of freedom among men was not a grant from a beneficent elite but was rather an inherent characteristic of each of the individual people as granted by that Creator. That nation is our own, these United States of America.

Over time, even here, a parasitical ruling class has ravaged the dignity of the individual and persistently violated not only the mere privileges doled out by those who are in fact simply public servants, but rather the unalienable human rights secured and granted by our Creator.

For more than ten decades this self appointed ruling class, globalists who have operated in the shadows, has dismantled the framework of limited government that had hitherto contained and restrained a ravenous beast that infiltrates and subverts cherished institutions.

This beast purchases the souls of men with crumbs from a cupboard stocked with booty and plunder. It warps them into complacent lap dogs that gratefully lick the boots of their leering masters. Those who should serve us instead increasingly enslave us.

We have observed inversions of common sense behavior and have watched incredulously as bizarre institutions have developed that justify abuse of liberty and property in the name of irrational and convoluted arguments.

Slaughter of the unborn is labeled choice; forced redistribution of wealth, clearly unadulterated theft, exists under a warped rubric of charitable works; our money has been methodically devalued; we import energy in the name of some green goddess despite vast reserves of natural resources; our nation's industrial base has been deliberately dismantled, we rely on basic necessities from those who would destroy us, and serious thinkers question the depths of depravity to which rampant abuse of power has perverted the actions and ethics of our government.

To what extent are we to tolerate this abuse? The Founders decided they would not tolerate far less than the treachery we have already allowed into our midst. Patrick Henry before the Second Virginia Convention in 1775 summed it up when he said,

> "...we shall not fight our battles alone. There is a just God who presides over the destinies of nations... Is life so dear, or peace so sweet, as to be purchased at the price of chains and slavery? Forbid it, Almighty God! I know not what course others may take; but as for me, give me liberty or give me death!"

Are we content to live in the chains of debt and bureaucratic bondage and the insufferable detritus of unfettered selfishness and entitlement sanctioned by wholesale compromises of our core values and traditions? Shall we be manhandled and sit by idly while our world is turned upside down by those who are ignorant of history and its lessons, or worse yet are aware and do not care? While we accept that we must and will be tolerant in a free society, shall we suffer assault from every quarter on truth itself? Is life so dear or peace so sweet? I think not.

Some people may be uncomfortable with this discussion. We hear the bromide of separation of church and state that is dribbled from those who have never read the Constitution or worse, have read it and find it "flawed". This essay is far too brief to attempt to cure that profound misunderstanding.

Here, we seek truth. May it stand on its own merit and may it speak to each man's heart. Believe each of us what we will, here is the relevance: without some skeleton upon which to drape the flesh of political reality, we stand emaciated and vulnerable to those predators whose raison d'être is to eviscerate the weak. Minds not adequately equipped with truth cannot withstand the cleverly contrived and twisted logic of those whose goal is simply to subjugate the willing, the emotionally weak, and the intellectually unprepared. They have thought out their position. So must we ours.

Are we to surrender the very freedom we were bequeathed by the Founders to those we elect to serve us?

16 - What Is The Role Of Public Servants?

"...that the Pleasure of doing Good and Serving their Country, and the Respect such Conduct entitles them to, are sufficient Motives with some Minds to give up a great Portion of their Time to the Public, without the mean Inducement of pecuniary Satisfaction."

Benjamin Franklin

"The liberties of a people never were, nor ever will be, secure, when the transactions of their rulers may be concealed from them."

Patrick Henry

There are many qualities one could consider regarding the role of public servants; however, three in particular are appropriate at this juncture. What is their vision? How do they view leadership? What is their understanding of the role and nature of The Law? We do not need to delve into laborious detail to incite a curiosity as to how a public servant's attitude affects his outlook about the power he wields and his relationship to those he serves.

Based on their dedication to principles, the Founders believed that individual liberty required a commitment to justice.[23] In an imperfect time and manner, they put in place a government that they hoped would tend toward the highest dreams of men. This is not new, but it is exactly to the extent to which what follows is commonly known that we can see the outworking of the Biblical perspective and the Founders' intent. In our times, men like Martin Luther King, Jr. have expressed it as a dream when men would be judged by the content of their character and not the color of their skin.

Paul Phaneuf

Leadership is service not domination. It is a higher calling, not a means to a selfish end. This vision of a Godly leader was exemplified by Jesus when He told His disciples that servanthood was the true measure of a leader.[24] A leader shares a common vision with those he serves. He runs tirelessly toward an objective, mindful of the witness of his fellow men and history.[25] He knows he leads because as he gives of himself to others he sees others following after him. Leaders do not lead from behind whipping the backs of those to whom they owe allegiance.

In a free society, leaders should be men of experience and character who will deal fairly and consistently with other men as their equals, not their rulers.[26]

True public servants of this Constitutional Republic acknowledge that lawful, limited government must ask two questions before imposing restrictive, intrusive, coercive, or confiscatory statutes upon its citizens.

First, they must determine with absolute certainty that only coercion can resolve a situation that possibly falls within government's purview. In other words, if a solution to any problem or challenge can be resolved by the voluntary actions of free individuals or institutions, then the rationalization for the use of force is proscribed. Force is only justified in defense of liberty, not in the enforcement of arbitrary regulations designed only to control people or to achieve agendas imposed on free people against their will by central planners.

The second question which is integral to the first, and which must be asked simultaneously and not sequentially is; does the Constitution even permit the Federal Government to insert itself into the equation? Is this a matter which the Constitution leaves to the people or the States?

It follows that public servants who value genuine Liberty acknowledge that law that violates the innate nature of man is invalid. Again there is a maxim that states that "Law is established for the benefit of men." The understanding here is that men must legislate in such a manner as to avoid violating the well being of other men. Scripture tells us that Christ set us free for the sake of freedom, and that we should not allow ourselves to be subject to a yoke of slavery.[27] Any statute that violates this scriptural edict is itself a violation of Law and thus has no standing.

These few examples are a tiny sample of the principles which we must insist our leaders respect. They were more than mere words to the Founders and to those of us who choose to live by them. They help us to stand tall in the gales of troubling times. We hope they will sustain us when we are challenged beyond our imagined capacities.

Given the insights we have just considered, it is reasonable to ask: Is freedom unlimited or are we constrained by a higher Law? We accept that under Natural Law, individuals in a civilized society must concede to some restrictions on personal liberty consistent with the protection of the rights of other men. However, if we are to nurture and protect freedom, we must necessarily also ask: is government itself subject to Law? That question is readily answered with a few observations.

First, if we the creators of government are subject to law then the creature we have designed must also be. Secondly, the Constitution states forthrightly, this Constitution shall be the Supreme Law of the Land. Government flows out of the words contained in the Founding documents and is subject to them. Finally, the notion that we are a nation of laws is rendered absurd if the government itself is rooted in lawlessness. Ultimately, government is nothing more than the behavior of the people who serve us as our employees. When the public servants in government ignore the Law, their behavior renders its dictums void and unenforceable and without authority or merit. We are not obligated to submit to lawless renegades.

This truth is not an excuse for abuse of the law by a constituent free people. The moving consideration is the government's own lawlessness, not arbitrariness on the part of the people. This raises a question we will now consider: Does freedom have limits?

17 - Does Freedom Have Limits?

"Bad men cannot make good citizens. A vitiated state of morals, a corrupted public conscience are incompatible with freedom."

Patrick Henry

"To grant that there is a supreme intelligence who rules the world and has established laws to regulate the actions of his creatures; and still to assert that man, in a state of nature, may be considered as perfectly free from all restraints of law and government, appears to a common understanding altogether irreconcilable. Good and wise men, in all ages, have embraced a very dissimilar theory. They have supposed that the deity, from the relations we stand in to himself and to each other, has constituted an eternal and immutable law, which is indispensably obligatory upon all mankind, prior to any human institution whatever. This is what is called the law of nature....Upon this law depend the natural rights of mankind."

Alexander Hamilton

What follows are a tiny sample of the hundreds of verses in the Bible that speak to Law, the nature of man, freedom, and the role of legitimate government. The consensus among men who accept the notion of a higher or "supernatural" authority is that there is an abundance of material to enable men to discern truths relevant to the matters we are considering. The Judeo Christian worldview declares that these truths are based on the very nature of God. In the Scriptures, God has promised that those who seek Him will find Him.[28] A reasonable corollary is that in knowing the nature of the Lawgiver, one may learn something of the nature of Law itself.

Paul Phaneuf

Here are just a few examples from the Bible. Again, regardless of one's belief system, for the Founders, the Scriptures were central to their lives and thoughts.

The very premise of a tripartite government comes from the Bible. In speaking of God, Isaiah says the Lord is "our judge, our lawgiver, and our king."[29] Here we have the model, in God's innate Being for the judiciary, the legislative, and the executive branches of our government. There are other verses that speak to this.

In his Gettysburg Address, Abraham Lincoln spoke of a government of the people, by the people, and for the people. What is not generally known is that these words were written by John Wycliffe, an early translator of the Bible who wrote in the General Prologue of his 1384 translation of the Bible that "The Bible is for the government of the people, by the people, for the people."

The concept of the Bible as a basis for law and governance was not new to Lincoln, or to the Founders. Wycliffe's thinking was that the Bible should be available to all men to read so as to enable them to arrange their own lives as they saw fit. The rationale for him was the same as it was for the Founding Fathers. Responsible men were capable of governing themselves if they lived according to the Bible's moral order.

The limits of freedom are also established scripturally in many places. The Bible tells us that though we are called to freedom, we should not turn our freedom into an excuse to do wrong, but rather through love we should serve one another.[30] We are also told that while we should act as free men, our freedom should not be a cover up or excuse for evil.[31]

The notion that God's commands are not capricious but rather point men to a life structured around the nature of man as God created him is found throughout Scripture. The Psalmist says in the Old Testament that while he will walk and enjoy his liberty, he will seek to do God's will. [32]

The end result of living according to Godly principles is found in these prophetic words in Isaiah. Note the enumeration of benefits to be derived as a result of the prophet's (and later, Jesus') obedience: that the spirit of the Lord was upon him because God had commissioned him to bring good news to those who are troubled. He sent him to comfort the broken hearted, to proclaim liberty and freedom to prisoners. [33]

We are told how to treat one another in a curious but profound verse that tells us to speak and act as though we will be judged by the "law of liberty". [34] What is the Law of Liberty? It is the requirement that men act according to moral principles as per the Ten Commandments but without the difficult burdensome regulations of daily life that were found in the Law of Moses. Jesus himself distilled the Ten Commandments down to two: Love God with all your heart, mind, and soul, and love your neighbor as yourself. [35]

Still some ask does it really matter what we think or believe.

That question is addressed at least in part with this final consideration. Ayn Rand, a professed atheist and the author of <u>Atlas Shrugged</u>, would have argued against any religious source as the basis for restrictions of personal liberty. Nevertheless she understood that prosperity was not possible if a society is immersed in anarchy and she approached the need for limits on freedom from the perspective of "rational selfishness".

While she would not recognize God as the source of a hierarchical structure of values to achieve a greater good that does not violate principles of liberty, she did in fact realize that unrestrained selfishness resulted in chaos. Thus even Rand concluded that if one is to have a society that yields peace, prosperity and liberty, freedom itself has to coexist with other objective values. She argued these other values could be determined through the use of reason.

Rand argued that while natural rights are absolutes and non negotiable, that is not to say that genuine Liberty is nothing more than unbridled self gratification. The Founders accepted the Judeo Christian values as their source for defining limits of appropriate personal expression and behavior, but even an avowed atheist like Ayn Rand understood that it is impossible to escape the necessity of some system that secures order within the framework of the unalienable rights of men.

One cannot escape the truth that freedom and Liberty are lived in the real world among other people and not in a theoretical vacuum. There is a tension between freedom and tyranny that has through most of recorded history favored tyranny and the enslavement of men by the State. We will consider this in the next chapter.

18 - Freedom or Tyranny?

"As a man is said to have a right to his property, he may be equally said to have a property in his rights. Where an excess of power prevails, property of no sort is duly respected. No man is safe in his opinions, his person, his faculties, or his possessions."

James Madison

Ripened fruit is sweet. Spoiled fruit is not edible, rots in place, draws flies and ferments in the belly. The fruits of freedom are as plain as both the unparalleled abundance our nation has produced, and the decline we have experienced over time as freedom has been compromised by out of control government.

Even as the spoilers have agonized at the insult of ordinary men elevated to the status of sovereigns by a God they cannot control; even as they have indulged their ravenous gluttony for the fruit of other men's labors; even as they have ravaged the affairs, the peace, the constructs of the shoddy serfs whose necks they seek to yoke; even through all of this, it has taken them over 100 years to bring us to the edge of destruction. So awesomely stable is the Judeo Christian foundation upon which this nation was built that it has endured their subterfuge and sabotage around the world. We are all that is left standing between them and their conquest of the human race.

It is trite, but it is true. The rising tide lifts all the boats. It is not trickled down, it is built upwards. It is not upon the backs of labor that honest and sincere men employ free enterprise to build empires. Rather it is upon the ideals, the

Paul Phaneuf

ideas, the risk, and the sweat of men who had dreams and provided innovation and jobs for those who preferred the security of employment rather than paying the personal cost of entrepreneurship.

It bears repeating that every system is infected with insincere and dishonest men. That is a reality of the human condition that we all must deal with so it is disingenuous to judge a system on the basis of how corrupt and selfish individuals distort it. This is true of socialism and free enterprise both. Any system must be judged on its merits and results.

That being the case, it is impossible not to see that the wreckage of socialism is visible, not just in history, but in our daily news. Can we not admit that those who would deny what is obvious, that socialism absolutely does not work, have an agenda that is only hidden from people who have chosen the path of least resistance, i.e., they choose to remain uninformed? It is those who are too mind numbed to lift their eyes and observe the obvious who deny it.

Can we admit that the socialist path to misery is established and well documented? Socialism's advocates do not praise its results, they ply their promises. It is their supposed uniqueness that will enable that which has never worked for others to magically deliver different results because of their superior abilities. In fact socialism's devastating consequences can no longer be questioned by serious thinkers. Surely, it is primarily those who have already resigned to the control of their lives by other persons who bow in submission at the feet of those who are at best their equals but are in fact only their servants.

Socialism is ultimately a system of State control of the economy. It has manifested in numerous forms throughout history. In the twentieth century it has expressed itself as

Communism, Marxism, Nazism, and Fascism. It has morphed from blatant political expression to social expression in the guise of social justice, environmentalism, etc. The common element to all of these is an aggregation of power to the State. Central planners, oligarchs, bureaucrats, or regulators all share a virtually limitless desire to control everything, and more importantly, everyone within their purview. Experience has shown that this appetite for power increases over time. In fact it is insatiable and permanent. The State rarely surrenders power it has accrued to itself.

One cannot control anything that affects the human condition without controlling the people themselves. Thus an ever present aspect of socialism, regardless of the cosmetics with which it dresses itself, is the fact that it is always about controlling, directing and restricting individuals. Inevitably it must become controlling people against their will, because people are not disconnected from their own self interest and do not voluntarily submit to demands that they have observed do them harm. Socialism and tyranny are intimates. Socialism and freedom are incompatible and mutually exclusive.

Daniel Webster wrote:

"Good intentions will always be pleaded for every assumption of authority. It is hardly too strong to say that the Constitution was made to guard the people against the dangers of good intentions. There are men in all ages who mean to govern well, but they mean to govern. They promise to be good masters, but they mean to be masters."

The nation that the Founders grounded on the principles of Scripture has never been equaled in its abundance and freedom since humanity was tossed outside of Eden.

What stands now between us and the nightmare envisioned by the cabal that seeks global dominance, which justifies theft in the name of charity, which elevates the planet to the status of goddess, and renders man as worth less than an owl? True Law does. Free men do. I do. Do you?

19 - Who Owns You?

"All positive and civil laws should conform, as far as possible, to the law of natural reason and equity."

"As neither reason requires nor religion permits the contrary, every man living in or out of a state of civil society has a right peaceably and quietly to worship God according to the dictates of his conscience."

Samuel Adams

Liberty can only exist long term among men and women who can answer this question to their own satisfaction: Who are you? By way of illustration, what follows is the answer that satisfies me when I ask the question of myself: Who am I?

I am a child of God, a unique and special creation of a God who has made me in His image and likeness and that He has made me like He is Himself. He has made me a free being and only God may claim ownership of me or you. Certainly no government may legitimately do so.

In a very real and substantive way, I am the king of my domain (as are you), under the Sovereign King of the universe. My domain is my body. I am soul, body, and spirit. My spirit is of God and energizes me. My soul is my mind, emotions, and consciousness; and my body is the vessel with which I move and through which I act in this world. Clearly, I am more than just my body. To be accurate, I consider my body to belong to God. I am a steward of what God has given to me, but as far as the government is concerned, my body is my property.

Paul Phaneuf

The products I produce with my labor, the creations of my intellect and imagination, the consequent wealth produced by my efforts are also my property. The same is true of the property of other sovereign individuals. I may not take from them what is theirs; they may not take from me what is mine; and neither of us may authorize another to do for us what we may not do ourselves, because it violates Natural Law. What is wrong for one sovereign individual to do to another is still wrong when two or more sovereign individuals act together.

God has established certain Laws under which I, the vassal king must live. I shall have no gods before Him; He is the King of kings. My first allegiance is to Him. I shall not bow to any other king or the symbol of any other king. I shall not even speak of such a betrayal.

My kingdom extends out to my family and I shall preserve it inviolate. I shall honor my father and my mother and shall teach my children the same. I shall not violate the family structure of another's kingdom and invade the sovereignty of that family by committing adultery with the spouse of another.

I shall respect all life and will not murder. This is a violation of the Law of my King of kings and a violation of the rights of other sovereign beings who are the kings, male and female, of their own bodies, their domains. This right to life includes all people, male and female, young and old, healthy or infirm, dying or in gestation.

I shall respect the rights and property of others. I shall not steal. I have no right to steal and therefore cannot confer that right upon any other person or entity in my name or on my behalf. This violates the Law of my King of kings (the Natural Rights of Man) and the Common Law.

I shall not bear false witness against my neighbor, the sovereign king of his domain. Such would be a violation of his or her person, reputation, property or liberty.

The King of kings' proscription against theft and the establishment of the sanctity of property are such that He forbids me to crave my neighbors house, or goods, or anything that is my neighbors.

And as He has clearly decreed that life shall be inviolable in the person of each individual that He has created, He has declared that the foundational unit of society is the family by ruling that, beyond the prohibition against adultery, I may not crave my neighbor's spouse.

I am to love Him with my whole heart, mind, strength and soul, and I am to treat my neighbor as I would have him treat me. This is not only His Law, but it is also deducible Natural Law as mutual respect is not only in my own interest but is in the best interest of the society I and my fellow man have constructed.

As such, it is a logical byproduct and a natural outworking of the Law of Love that I shall practice charity; that I shall help those less fortunate than myself; that I shall seek to live with integrity and a sense of gratitude; that I shall respect others and act honorably toward them; that I shall seek to make things right where I have erred and make amends to those whom I have wronged; that I shall always walk with humility and recognize that I do not know all things and may learn from everyman who walks according to the Laws of Nature and the Laws of the Creator.

These are the true Laws that govern the domain of my personal space, the space where my existence manifests by the presence of my body, that property which is the gift of my Creator and in which my soul has resided and matured.

Do you believe it is possible to be sovereign under God without being lawless? Can free and sovereign men unite under a social compact that promotes peace and order without compromising liberty? We already did. How?

20 - What Do You Tell the World?

"I know but one code of morality for men, whether acting singly or collectively. He who says I will be a rouge when I act in company with a hundred others, but an honest man when I act alone, will be believed in former assertion, but not in the latter... if the morality of one man produces a just line of conduct in him, acting individually, why should not the morality of one hundred men produce a just line of conduct in them, acting together?"

Thomas Jefferson

I am a free, sovereign individual who seeks to live free and peacefully among and with other sovereign individuals. Every human being is a sovereign individual and is the property of neither any other human nor, and especially concerning these United States of America, of any government.

I and my family, with others, together "We the People," have compacted to form a government among men to establish a more perfect union; a government that shall be restrained and empowered only to "...establish Justice, insure domestic Tranquility [among the sovereign states], provide for the common defense, promote [not provide] the general welfare, and secure the Blessings of Liberty to ourselves and Our Posterity." True Liberty precludes legal plunder even in the name of good intentions. Also, said federal government shall guarantee a republican form of government for every State.[36]

Furthermore, "...in order to prevent misconstruction or abuse of its powers, [in order to]...best ensure the beneficent ends of its institution... [we do hereby] add further declaratory and restrictive clauses..."[37] to powers granted to the federal government. No implied permissions extending the power of this servant government may be construed, nor can any obedience to said unlawful appropriation of powers be expected or required under any moral or ethical standards, despite claims to the contrary by beneficiaries of these power grabbers.

In fact any such usurpation of power shall constitute an infringement upon the rights of man and "We the People" shall defend those God given rights and liberties and if necessary dissolve this union in order that we may choose whatever form of government is consonant with the Laws of Nature and Nature's God.[38] As free men we pledge not to fail or neglect our duties so as to avoid precipitating the need to resort to this most undesirable alternative. Save us from that necessity, Almighty God!

This federal government may not establish a national religion, nor prohibit the free exercise thereof; nor abridge freedom of speech nor of the press; nor of "We the People" to peaceably assemble or petition our [servant] government for a redress of grievances.[39]

Nor may it infringe upon our right to bear arms[40], an extension of our right to live free and protect our persons, our families, our property, and our liberty.

We shall be secure in our persons, homes, papers, and effects[41]. We may not be compelled to testify against ourselves, nor be deprived of life, liberty or property without due process of law, nor without just compensation[42].

We may only be convicted by a jury of our peers[43] as is consistent with our sovereignty, the Law of the King of kings, and common and natural law.

"We the People" shall be the final arbiters of fact and law[44] and do retain the power and authority to declare any unconscionable or unconstitutional law as null and void by our refusal as jurors to convict according to our conscience.[45]

The enumeration of certain rights shall not be construed by our servant government as to deny or disparage other unalienable rights retained by us and which our Creator may have also granted.[46] Any powers not specifically delegated or enumerated in our compact nor prohibited by it to the servant States are reserved to the servant States and to The Sovereign People. These limits shall not be ignored by this servant federal government. "We the People" shall perform our duty and stringently protect and defend our liberties against encroachment or dissolution even to the tiniest degree by our public servants.

As the sovereign of my domain under the King of kings, I do hereby declare and proclaim my individual liberty and renounce any interpretation or understanding which would otherwise invert the status between me and the creation of my fellow sovereigns of a servant government for the purposes announced in our Constitution and for no other purposes.

In fact I do hereby proclaim, under that same authority and before all men that any actions by that servant government outside of the specific powers granted to it are not in fact law but merely the color of law[47], such statutes, regulations, and rules being in fact unlawful; that they shall be null and void and unenforceable, and I do hereby publicly repudiate them.

Those public servants who would subvert this government to their own selfish ends and act outside the authority of those powers enumerated in the Constitution of these

United States shall be guilty of crimes against the people, and the Law of Nature and Nature's God and shall be acting in violation of their oaths to protect and defend that Constitution.

Morally, logically, Constitutionally, and of necessity to maintain respect for the rule of law, the servant government or its agents may not act outside the law, may not exempt themselves from the law, may not act under color of law, nor can they ever be above the law. In so doing they exhibit contempt for those they serve and for the Law itself and demonstrate by their behavior that they are the enemies of God, of True Law, of the people and their created institution the State, and of the Constitution.

Do you not have a right to claim your own body? Do you not own yourself, subject to your Creator? Are you not Sovereign Under God?

21 - What Are Your Answers?

What do I believe? I believe that there is overwhelming spiritual and historical evidence which is available even to people who would disagree with my personal convictions that the Judeo Christian scripture and its moral teachings are the basis of our civilization, and consequently, I can stand on what it teaches, act on what it demands with confidence, and thereby order my life and allegiance according to its dictates.

I believe that I answer first to God and my conscience, and that I have the responsibility to ensure that the institution of government, which I and my fellow sovereigns have created to serve and protect us, does not act in violation of the very powers and principles of Nature and Nature's Law to which we are ourselves subject. That supervising the servant institutions to which we have entrusted the use of force is of primary concern, as it is proven in history that the use of force is quickly perverted and turned against the master when in the hands of selfish men, and that the progress toward this end is inevitable unless it is actively opposed.

Paul Phaneuf

I believe that we find ourselves in that position today. That the monstrous debt, the overreaching bureaucracy, the confiscatory and complex tax code, the onerous and intrusive regulations that do not facilitate commerce but seek to control it, the excessive compensation and privileges which our servants have granted to themselves, the power of lobbyists to purchase not just favors but the very consciences of our public servants point to a state of emergency that can only be resolved by a groundswell of sovereign men and women asserting their lawful authority over the subservient instrumentalities which we through our forefathers have constructed.

It is time to cage the beast. That is best achieved by informing the minds of our fellow sovereigns. Truth is the disinfectant that will wash away the slime of liberalism that now pollutes our seriously ill, supposedly servant government, and has swelled it with the nauseating pus of authoritarianism.

I have just told you who I am, what I believe and why I believe it. I have shared my paradigm. It is my motivating beacon. It is the light toward which I strive. I answer to God first, to conscience. I am ever aware of my imperfections but I cannot allow the perfect to stand in the way of the better and will not turn away from that which is right merely because I may on occasion err. Next my loyalty is to family, then community, then state, then and lastly, to my country. The federal government is not my country. It is the tool we use to oversee the defense of our country and that tool exists to protect our liberties.

Let me qualify that placing the federal government last is not derisive. It is a hierarchy into which I have allowed only elements about which I in fact care deeply. It is not that I have no loyalty to the federal apparatus. It is simply that the federal apparatus is most remote and unresponsive to me and represents thereby the greatest threat among those elements that I allow into my sovereign kingdom.

Remember, we bow only to God and stand on a level plane with our fellow men. All the "stuff" we make, invent, or create resides on a field that we as sovereign beings under God look down upon like doting parents. We are the masters, intended by God from the beginning to have dominion[48], overseeing His creation as his caretakers and stewards. We have no intention of genuflecting to "stuff," or to men who demand that we take a knee before them or to their "stuff."

And to those who would argue that God has ordained governments among men,[49] it is not blind submission that God requires. Scripture makes clear that we "submit" (cooperate with) government only if it:

Is itself under the authority (Laws) of God.

Punishes wrongdoing and not that which is good

Ministers to (is a servant of) citizens not their master (God's role)

Is not arbitrary or inconsistent, but rather true to principle

Restrains itself strictly within the confines of the social compact which is enshrined in its founding documents

In fact honors God (the Creator who has granted unalienable rights)

Exists for God's purposes (is itself subject to the Laws of Nature...)

That being said, and within that context, I do in fact love my country and am proud of our heritage and believe that we are the greatest country to occupy the face of the earth because our Founders sought to found this nation upon Godly principles. I am proud that we learn from our mistakes and have sought to rectify injustice. I am ashamed that "We the People" have grown fat, lazy, self indulgent and stupid. If this offends you, prove me wrong.

And as Jesus taught, how great is the darkness when we call the darkness light?[50] It is a great misfortune to have to exist in the darkness, but it is a march to extinction to be unaware that light exists and fail to seek its efficacious benefits once we are alerted.

I am quite aware that what I have written will bring me scorn from many quarters. I have not written these pages on impulse, neither have I written them to be popular or beloved by men of power.

I am compelled to cry out from the darkness that is enveloping and devouring us.

I expect to pay a price. I stand in opposition to those who would be our masters. So be it.

This book is my declaration. Behold, there is a light. We are not lost. The darkness is a choice.

So, with respect, I ask and shall continue to ask:

Who are you?

What do you believe?

Why do you believe it?

PART TWO

PURPOSE

"The question before the human race is, whether the God of nature shall govern the world by his own laws, or whether priests and kings shall rule it by fictitious miracles."

John Adams

22 - So What?

"I am only one, but I am one. I cannot do everything, but I can do something. And because I cannot do everything, I will not refuse to do the something that I can do. What I can do, I should do. And what I should do, by the grace of God, I will do."

Edward Everett Hale

Whenever I do an inquiry of this type I always approach it with the attitude that I could have been doing something else with my time like drinking beer or taking a nap. If you are thinking of doing that now and have survived to this point, I implore you to stay with me a little while longer.

I ask the question, so what? So we have looked at the influence of the Founders' worldview. I have shared my insights and opinions. We have considered the nature of freedom, the role of government, the nature of man, the condition of our Republic and considered many other ideas.

So what? If ideas become like big books that sit and collect dust on people's end tables or stand unopened on the shelves of an impressive looking but useless library, why bother?

For me the next step is action. The only way that a nation founded upon the enduring principles that our Founders applied can end up as a petty bureaucracy, with a devalued currency and underutilized natural resources, a third rate educational system, an apathetic public that does not vote; and a Congress that does not respect the rule of Law is if the people of that nation have forgotten or are ignoring everything important.

Paul Phaneuf

Now some might argue that I have not made the case to specify the abuses enumerated in this manuscript. The simple fact is America is a mess.

Evidence of this is demonstrated by the Presidential election in 2008. Americans elected a man to the Oval Office who can sing a tune and swing a golf club. Because he had a fluent delivery and is bi-racial, he was able to capitalize on the angst of a nation that was looking to put racial divides behind them. He was the wrong man.

He has been an arrogant and incompetent fraud who exposes his character by incessantly repeating a lie, seemingly believing that by doing so it will become true. He has pontificated foolishness as though it were wisdom. He is symptomatic of the progressive epidemic that has infected the federal government for a century.

And because we have allowed those self same brokers of power who have no respect for truth and American values to mold a generation of children in their Orwellian educational ghettos, we have a generation that lacks discernment and believes unthinkingly. We have gotten the leader we deserve and a liberal main stream media that is his ticky-tacky lackey mouthpiece. God help us.

It is my intention that this should be a book that is written not to speak to the news of the day, or even the mindset of our decade, but one that would speak to timeless truths. The fact is that as of this writing in 2012 ours is a nation in decay and we are headed for the dustbins of history.

Where once despite our flaws we were a great nation because of our principles, we are now the world's greatest debtor. Our lawless government has through ignominious statutes ignored the supreme law of the land and has rendered our currency into worthless paper. The Congress has abdicated its responsibility to coin money and regulate the value thereof.[51] We conduct commerce not with specie based on gold and silver but with fiat currency based on debt unlawfully issued by a cabal of private bankers who charge us interest to lend us money they have created out of thin air.[52] They are not even accountable to Congress.[53]

Oh, the hideous betrayal! We were once the engine of industry for the world, we were the most desirable nation in which to do business, we were innovators, and we were respected. Now we act as though we are nothing but a shiny veneer covering an enormous rot. Our allies do not trust us and our enemies laugh behind our backs while looking at a picture of the President as he bowed from the waist before a foreign king.

None of us are inclined to commit to any cause without sufficient prospects of progress or improvement. It is not unreasonable to ask, so what? We would need another book to expose all the sources of the stench that exudes from the corruption that has polluted the Founders' noble experiment. Here are a few reasons to motivate us to return to basic principles:

so we can come to our senses; so that we can awaken those who are still asleep; so that we can take back our children and prepare the next generation; so that we can reinstitute sound money; so that we can get back to basics; so that we can pass on the dream of liberty;

so that we can remove any office holder from his or her cushy job if they do not understand their role as public servants; so that we can insist that those who hold public office have read the Constitution; so that we can take our country back and try, with all our might, on our knees begging God for help, to save freedom for our children; so that we can prevent national bankruptcy;

so that we might once again be respected in the world because we understand our roots; so that we can right the wrongs we have allowed politicians to perpetrate; so that we can return to the notion of citizen legislators, not crooks who vote themselves a lifetime income because they serve a few years in a high paying, high profile government position;

so that we can elect legislators who place themselves under the same laws by which they attempt to bind us;

so that we can have real hope based on substantive truths, not on the empty promises of windbags; so that we can end tyranny with a happy face; so that we can end the nanny state; so we can grow and prosper;

so that we can end the perpetual cycle of police actions, wars not constitutionally declared by Congress; so that we can survive and thrive; so that we can live principled lives; so that we do not have to be embarrassed at what we have become;

so that we can elect statesmen and not political hacks;

so that through our example we can demonstrate to the world the benefits of a Constitutional Republic...

Please, take a moment and fill in the blanks as I have barely scratched the surface. What would motivate you to act?

So that ______________________, and

So that______________________, and

So that ______________________, and...

How did we come to this place where the government is the ringmaster and we are the clowns and caged tigers in its circus?

23 - What Radical Inversion?

"If free governments, the rulers are the servants, and the people their superiors and sovereigns."
Benjamin Franklin

"Government is not reason, it is not eloquence, it is force. Like fire it is a dangerous servant and a fearsome master."
George Washington

The proper order of hierarchy is God, Man, Family, and government. God, Man (and Woman) and Family are capitalized because they are organic and Man and Family (when God created Woman) were directly created by God. This is a subjective decision by me. Now there are those who will argue that government is created by God and I concede that this is a true statement. But God's government is perfect. Those which He has ordained through men have all been, well, less than perfect.

Now for a coloring book recap of history; check the resources at the end of this volume for in depth history books:

Originally when our country began (ignoring the native inhabitants who in the history of humankind have always suffered when more advanced or militant civilizations invaded their land, and keeping in mind that ultimately, all men, regardless of where they live are emigrant exiles from Eden) men gathered in communities and formed local governments. When "We the People" rebelled from the colonial, monarchical, absolutist, statist tyrant, we declared that the basis of the rebellion was to protect unalienable rights that come from our Creator.

Various people squabble over all kinds of collateral arguments about who was represented by whom and whether or not this or that group was included in the Founding documents. Perhaps there is truth to these concerns. However, what is the purpose of that debate? The reality is each generation must claim and recommit to freedom. At this point in history, meaning now, the declaration is made that all men are endowed by their Creator with certain unalienable rights. That is where we are and where we make our stand.

Unalienable Rights, rights that cannot be taken from us without destroying us, predate any and all social compacts. It is academic what the intentions were of any group of men who invoke them. In declaring a social compact based on the Laws of Nature and Nature's God they publicly submitted themselves and their compact to a higher authority. In doing so, regardless of their intentions, they invited that higher authority as the standard and arbiter of their compact.

The Laws of Nature and Nature's God cannot be limited by the convenient intent of mere men. As such, the social compact extends to us all. It is arguable from their writings that the Founders' relied on this truth and believed that with time, the Declaration of Independence and the Constitution would tend by its reliance on the Laws of the Creator to minimize the abuses and shortcomings of their own efforts and the efforts of their posterity.

Furthermore, it being established that most men acknowledge some kind of Creator, it is understood by men like us that rights do not come from government. We can argue details forever.

Here is the point. I am a man. I was not created by government. Governments were created by a being superior to them, that is, men (and women) like me (that is living humans) who are born free and intend to live that way or die fighting to stay or become that way; who were themselves subject to the highest authority, God. If this is not sufficiently uncomplicated then please feel free to join the ranks of those who want to spend their days debating the number of angels that can dance on the head of a pin.

The Founders, whose ancestors had initially formed local communities, were originally organized into colonies from one national government or another, primarily England, and eventually organized into States under the Articles of Confederation. The People, who were imperfect, who eventually formed the republican states, which were imperfect, sent representatives, who were imperfect, who formed a federal government, which was imperfect, which was limited by a Constitution, which was imperfect (not flawed), so that people like you and me, who are imperfect, could be free. Is that not sufficiently clear if historically imperfect? It is not complicated.

Let me clarify for a moment my observation that while the Constitution was imperfect, it was not flawed. The notion of being imperfect acknowledges the obvious fact that having been written by men for men, the document would necessarily not be perfect. The notion of flawed implies that it is structurally, foundationally, inherently incorrect as a concept. No, the Constitution may be imperfect but it is not "flawed".

Continuing the former point: the proper order of government is God, over Man (and Family), over Local and State, all of them over the Federal government.

Here is the radical inversion:

Somehow we have been duped, over time, into believing that the pecking order has been reversed. Now it is the Federal (national) government, over State and local, over Man and family, and down at the bottom, subservient to all is the Creator of the universe; lower than low, once declared by a national publication to be dead[54]; now supposedly separated from government; and even when simply the expression of spiritual sentiment by a private citizen, now banned throughout the entire public sector by some kind of giant, humongous, insurmountable, really, really big, giant but curiously invisible wall.

It is the Wall of Walls behind which we are protected from a horrible fiend. Particularly heinous and ostracized is the Name of Jesus Christ. Here in this tiny place we find none other than that Almighty God who is exactly referred to as such in 30 of the 50 State Constitutions. All fifty States reference God in their Constitutions. Behind that supposed wall is relegated that Creator who is recognized in the Declaration of Independence, and that Lord referenced in the date of the signing in Article VII of the United States Constitution. Wow. How did this happen?

Were it not for the fact that the Creator of the universe is Omnipotent, and it is from Him that we have acquired, as a gift mind you, our freedom, this would be laughable. As it is, the entire thing is incredibly alarming and awful, and disturbingly, people who are just like those responsible for this fiasco are actually in charge of our nation. What have we done? And we wonder why the world and America is a pathetic mess?

This inversion is a giant fraud. It has to be.

How else does the top become the bottom and the bottom becomes the top except by deceit and subterfuge?

How has that which by nature is the greatest become the least?

How has that which has been created become superior to its creator?

How has the servant become the master?

How has the potter come to be molded by the clay?

In what insane asylum does this folly exist?

In America, God forbid. In America, God help us. And upon what fulcrum has the lever been placed which has inverted the natural order of the universe?

On the fulcrum of lies! By calumny! By thievery! By coercion! By betrayal! By apathy! By neglect! By stupidity! By cowardice! By laziness!

Who will ring the alarm? Where is our midnight rider? Who will weep for us? Who will fight for us? No one, I tell you, no one. It is us. It is you and I or it is no one! We must fight for us.

Shame! Shame! How do we sleep at night knowing that we have sold our children into slavery?

I weep for America. Let us weep together for one moment. Then let us look to the future; let us be resolved; let us fight for our freedom. God willing we may yet be able to free our children from bondage.

How do we deal with this? Are the socialists right? Is freedom really nothing more than every man for himself? Can we have real freedom, genuine individual liberty, without degenerating into anarchy?

24 - What About Anarchy?

"As the cool and deliberate sense of the community ought in all governments, and actually will in all free governments ultimately prevail over the views of its rulers; so there are particular moments in public affairs, when the people stimulated by some irregular passion, or some illicit advantage, or misled by the artful misrepresentations of interested men, may call for measures which they themselves will afterwards be the most ready to lament and condemn. In these critical moments, how salutary will be the interference of some temperate and respectable body of citizens, in order to check the misguided career, and to suspend the blow mediated by the people against themselves, until reason, justice and truth, can regain their authority over the public mind?"

James Madison, Federalist No. 163, 1788

There is need for a moment of reflection here. Unbridled passion, even in the cause of liberty can lead to excesses. Now let us be clear that there is no room for compromise when it comes to freedom, and one man's extremism is another man's surrender.

Any ground lost to those who do not respect liberty and property must be retaken, but we have primarily lost ground by default; by assent through silence; by lack of vigilance and resolution. This is territory that has not so much been taken from us but rather surrendered by us.

It may require patience and time to recover; but here in America, as it was not lost primarily to direct violence, it does not require violence to recover it. We have been defrauded, not defeated. We have not lost our liberty in

Paul Phaneuf

battle, which is how it was initially obtained for us by the Founders; rather we have lost our liberty through neglect.

We will recover it by methods better suited to the means initially employed by those adversaries and opponents of liberty who have taken it from us. Here in our country, they robbed and defrauded us while we slumbered in a lazy stupor.

Violence is not called for unless those who now possess the power over us would turn to violence to keep it. This may occur, and in isolated cases, it has overtly appeared. And we must be alert to a subtle kind of violence that is routinely used by government on a daily basis: the powers of intimidation, incarceration, and confiscation.

The government has reached a point where it assumes to itself ever expanding powers and it is understandable that many patriots have lost not only patience but even the hope that we can ever recover the reins of self government without force. We must be cognizant and honest brokers of reason and analysis and admit that in the end, it could come to that.

However, the Founders paid the blood price so that we would not have to. They ratified the Bill of Rights for a reason. The greatest strength of the second amendment is its power as a deterrent. In WWII the emperor of Japan overruled the advice of his generals to invade the United States because he noted that when they landed on our shores they would encounter a rifle behind every blade of grass. We are an armed people. The goal is peace through strength.

"We the People" are strong. If the government tries to disarm us, a violent outcome is entirely predictable. Very few armed Americans would surrender their weapons to a government so committed to tyranny that it would violate the Second Amendment.

As has been stated already, the Second Amendment does not create the right to self defense, it affirms and protects it. The powers that be (or would be) are well served to be reminded: do not attempt to abrogate our right to keep and bear arms. That is the line in the sand that every patriot recognizes is the prelude to absolute tyranny. It will not be tolerated.

Be forewarned, you who would steal our liberty by subjecting our national sovereignty to the incompetent, fiendish United Nations. We have fallen asleep but we are not dead. There will be no blue helmets taking our guns, even if they paint their helmets green. The demands of conscience require that the sovereign free men of this nation will not submit to international treaties which subvert the Supreme Law of the Land, the United States Constitution, or compromise the Laws of Nature and Nature's God. Servant legislators should consider themselves on notice.

While the corruption in government is extensive, their power is not absolute, at least not yet. We still have the tools the Founders put in place to resolve our issues without violence.

As some have noted with alarm, it is true that the voting process has been corrupted, but it has not been dismantled. We are approaching a precipice, but until we have exhausted the peaceful measures available to us, talk of violence is not an appropriate response, at least not yet.

We have time to rise as a thinking free people. It is not time to rise as a violent people. But admittedly, the time is short. We have no time to waste waiting for someone else to act.

It is we who must engage in the weapons of peace while they are still available. What reason would we have to be optimistic of the outcome if we have to resort to the weapons of war against our own government on our own land? This time, it will not turn out well.

Why would the hand of Providence bless the actions of desperate men, who lost freedom because they were too self-indulgent to protect it after it had been handed to them as a gift? If we get to that point, it speaks to the degenerate condition of our character, and we will not have the fortitude it takes to win.

We must pray for God's blessing now. We must turn to the principled behavior that is necessary now. We must do what it takes while we can do it peaceably now.

What delusion would anyone profess that would find men who are insufficient to the cause while it can be done bloodlessly, to suddenly find the moral integrity to do what it takes when the sacrifice required would be so much greater? Is this not folly? The time to do the right thing is now.

What is the potential for victory, and what honor is there in dying because we were profoundly stupid? And someone please tell me, what switch will somebody pull to suddenly awaken minds so obtuse that we could not see the lights of the train that was bearing down on us in a darkened tunnel?

Freedom and license are antagonists, mutually exclusive like matter and antimatter. The one renders the other inoperable and where license is (a false freedom that is unbridled self indulgence, unrestrained by morals, mores, or ethics), genuine liberty is not.

Likewise, freedom and anarchy cannot be companions. Anarchy is the antithesis of order. It is bedlam, the survival not of the fittest but of the most ruthless. Anarchy is what happens when freedom is compromised. It grows when government becomes the nanny and starts telling people what they may or may not do with their own bodies, lives, and property. Anarchy is, among other things, free markets driven underground where they hide from legitimate rule of law; where greed, not ambition decides who rises to the top.

It is ironic that governments cause black markets and underground economies when they abuse liberty, then use the anarchy which inevitably develops as the excuse to further restrict law abiding, honest citizens; all the while the underground economy digs a little deeper, gets more profitable, more violent and then begins to infiltrate the government that created it with bribes. It is a vicious circle that is readily recognizable but by then, the money is seductive and the infiltration into the now corrupted government is difficult to eradicate.

That being said, there is another expression of anarchy which we must address. It is the anarchy of those who are lawless. They honor no law. Even if the government did not create a black market by its intrusive legalistic forays in violation of true law, these monsters would find a way to profit from lawlessness by creating victims for the sake of gain: kidnappers, cheats, thieves, slavers, predators. These are in fact the legitimate targets of lawful government. These anarchists do not seek free markets. They wantonly hurt people and take from others simply because they think they can.

They can be terrorist ideologues like the radical Islamofascists who believe that their god insists that they cut off the heads of infidels and demand tribute from their victims if they hope to be spared. Or they may be base extortionists, cowards who take simply because they do not fear opposition or consequences. Sometimes they are simply fiends who prey on the weak. But they are those against whom men of peace have banded together and formed governments for their common defense.

It is because of men like these, both in and out of government that we must have the ability to defend ourselves. Violent individuals are the proper objects of public servants who are true peace officers. The peace officers who serve us cannot be everywhere and can often only respond after the damage is done. This cannot be repeated too frequently: our right of self defense is unequivocal and unalienable. Our attitude toward any government that seeks to infringe upon our right of self defense must be one of absolute zero tolerance.

Regarding those men who would abuse power from within government, there are those who would argue that government has the right to regulate the type of "arms" that responsible free men may own. They put themselves in opposition to the vision of the Founders. Noah Webster wrote,

"Tyranny is the exercise of some power over a man, which is not warranted by law, or necessary for the public safety. A people can never be deprived of their liberties, while they retain in their own hands, a power sufficient to any other power in the state."

An armed people with power sufficient to stand up to a tyrannical government is not synonymous with anarchy. Laws restricting the right to keep and bear arms for the public safety are not the same as catering to unpredictable public paranoia. The notion of public safety applies to weapons in the hands of men who are insane, or who have no regard for the rights of their fellow man. While we cannot always know with certainty the motivations of those who would disarm us, we can know with certainty what the inevitable result will be. Tyranny!

Continuing, one finds that there are the anarchists who are well intentioned patriots but who cause harm to the cause by their premature resort to violence. They give up on the way of peace too soon and miss the opportunity to ride the rising tide of resistance. We cannot question their love of the America they seek to restore, but we can question their judgment.

This is one of many threats that out of control government introduces into the society. Men assess danger to themselves differently. When government has become the primary instrument of lawlessness, who can say with certainty where the line of self defense should be drawn?

We know that we face the unhappy possibility that there may come a time when we need to defend our liberty with violence. That time is not yet here. But when men believe they are under attack, who shall declare that they are absolutely wrong in their analysis of the threat? Men of character dread, deplore, and denounce violence; yet it is our responsibility to be prepared, to be armed, and to be willing, but we should not be eager.

That being said, we must be alert. As of this writing, in the year of Our Lord 2012, our servant government has now declared the following to be possible "terrorists" groups:

The Tea Party Movement, which is composed primarily of peaceful middle aged and senior citizens who want limited, Constitutional government and the debt and national deficit brought under control;

Former and current military and police personnel who have joined the "Oath Keepers", a group of individuals who have reaffirmed their sworn oaths to "protect and defend the Constitution from all enemies, foreign and domestic";

Christians (of course, we deny that the government is our god);

Patriot groups (even if firmly opposed to violence) are potentially "Homegrown terrorists";

Our Veterans are on the list of "possible terrorists" as are pro second amendment groups, supporters of traditional marriage and the right to life, and Americans who oppose any global government that would compromise American sovereignty.

Clearly the terrorism that we must fear most is the terrorism of Tyranny. To those who cherish freedom, it is evident that the federal government is out of control. The Founding Fathers must be spinning like high speed lathes in their graves!

Thomas Jefferson once wrote that the tree of liberty must be watered from time to time with the blood of patriots and tyrants.[55] That comment can potentially be misapplied and in the heart and mind of the undisciplined, or the overly enthusiastic, or the passionate idiot, it can be misunderstood and lead to more harm than good. Jefferson was not a man of violence. His comment without context appears to resound with the ring of inevitability. To interpret Jefferson's comments as a call to periodic bloodshed as some preventative ritual is nonsense.

Jefferson was speaking to historical truth but he was not suggesting an imminent inevitability. His observation is for us a profound and urgent warning. His generation could not avoid a war for liberty, but they provided us with tools with which we could. Our generation can and should avoid another armed revolution to secure our liberty. But our freedoms have been almost mortally compromised and we must restore them. The question is, will we?

What chance do we have to regain our freedom? Cannot the government crush even lawful remonstrations using the military?

25 - Is Our Military a Threat?

"A standing military force, with an overgrown Executive will not long be safe companions to liberty. The means of defense against foreign danger have been always the instruments of tyranny at home. Among the Romans it was a standing maxim to excite a war, whenever a revolt was apprehended. Throughout all Europe, the armies kept up under the pretext of defending, have enslaved the people."

James Madison

"Should this [combination between the executive and the legislative, in some scheme of usurpation] at any time happen, how easy would it be to fabricate pretenses of approaching danger! Indian hostilities, instigated by Spain or Britain, would always be at hand. Provocations to produce the desired appearances might even be given to some foreign power, and appeased again by timely concessions. If we can reasonably presume such a combination to have been formed, and that the enterprise is warranted by a sufficient prospect of success, the army, when once raised, from whatever cause, or on whatever pretext, may be applied to the execution of the project."

Alexander Hamilton

"Before a standing army can rule, the people must be disarmed; as they are in almost every kingdom in Europe. The supreme power in America cannot enforce unjust laws by the sword; because the whole body of the people are armed, and constitute a force superior to any band of regular troops that can be, on any pretense, raised in the United States. A military force, at the command of Congress, can execute no laws, but such as the people perceive to be just and constitutional; for they will possess the power, and jealousy will instantly inspire the inclination, to resist the execution of a law which appears to them unjust and oppressive."

Noah Webster

Paul Phaneuf

Never ending wars; collusion between the Executive Branch and Congress; a Congress that fails to protect its Legislative prerogatives; a bloated Executive; do these sound familiar? The Founders were not so much prescient as that they possessed an astute knowledge of history.

One factor that is a great encouragement to me is that our military swears an oath to "support and defend the Constitution against all enemies, foreign and domestic, that I will bear true faith and allegiance to the same..." The notion of true faith carries great significance and speaks to the conscience of the man and the sense of the real meaning of the Constitution.

The Nazis carried out unspeakable atrocities in the name of obedience to the commands of barbaric men. One would hope that swearing true faith to the Constitution would preclude obeying orders that break the Laws of Nature and Nature's God that the Declaration of Independence addresses.

A man of conscience must be willing to suffer the consequences for allegiance to the "true faith" of the Constitution. This requires discernment and courage. On the one hand, no military can function without disciplined soldiers willing to carry out dangerous missions in difficult circumstances; however, liberty will not long be sustained when a nation's military has crossed the line from well trained, fierce, and courageous warriors into heartless monsters. There is a difference. There may be controversy among people about specific circumstances and where the line is, but we all admit that there is a line that may not be crossed without turning us into the savages we supposedly revile.

Let us not be deceived, however. This is no guarantee that our "standing army" will not be used against us. There have been unfortunate instances of government using our military against American civilians: the slaughter of the Branch Davidians outside Waco, Texas in 1993 being only one example.

However, the military are our own sons and daughters, mothers and fathers, brothers and sisters, and we trust that they understand that it is their duty to defend our liberties, including our right to keep and bear arms, and we hope that they would be highly reluctant to abuse their fellow citizens without great consternation. Likewise, we must be alert to any attempts by our Federal Government to allow foreign troops on our homeland to "enforce" our laws, or even more insidiously, to enforce international laws. No international law governs Americans on our own soil. No International Treaty that compromises American sovereignty, our Constitution, or Natural Law is valid. That is a line we cannot allow our public servants to cross.

Can we not hope that there are many generals who would refuse an order to go against the American people without enormous self reflection and honest soul searching, and a clear conviction that the order was absolutely constitutional? The military answers directly to the Commander in Chief, a civilian. Nevertheless, the Commander in Chief of our military ought not to dare stray too far from the limits of his authority as imposed by the Constitution.

The American military is not the President's personal army. They are not Saddam Hussein's Inner Republican Guard. While the military affirms that they will obey the orders of the Commander in Chief, the oath they take is not an oath of loyalty to the man who occupies the office, but to the Constitution.

However, since 9/11/01, in the name of protecting us from terrorism, which is a legitimate responsibility of the Federal and State governments, many laws have been passed which should give us pause.[56] There has been a heated dialog as to what the government may or may not do to us in the name of "for us." It is a conundrum that our enemies have deliberately fostered upon us.

The enemies of Western civilization, among them radical Islamists, have no compunction to abuse our commitment to freedom by using it against our need to defend ourselves and defeat them. They are unrestrained by any civilized code. Encouraged by their radical ideology they are willing to sacrifice their lives committing acts of savagery.

Because nothing happens in isolation, we must observe that everything goes back to some uninvited and unlawful intrusion of government's camel nose into Liberty's tent. In this instance, many knowledgeable Americans point out that certain military excursions might have been avoided had we the sovereign people acted with greater wisdom and foresight.

For example, had we not allowed the federal government to usurp unto itself the power to obstruct our right to pursue energy independence here at home, how much less might we have needed to send our military personnel to the Middle East to secure needed energy resources? It is a fair question to ask, and we must accept responsibility for not controlling our public servants.

The Founders knew and feared what we are now experiencing. It is a perversion that our cherished and precious brethren in the armed forces have been utilized as an arm of a government that has escaped the chains that bind it, and we as a nation have allowed our fellow citizens to suffer the consequences of political wars.

There has been a blurring of the lines between adventurism, or military action necessitated because of the stupidity of our elected servants, and genuine war required to keep us safe. We as a people have been too busy playing games to supervise our public servants and have failed to replace certified imbeciles who were re-elected because of the inertia of incumbency and our inexcusable neglect.

The Constitution makes our military an arm of the people. This is not sophism. It is a distinction that is very real. It may be subtle, but it is not unrecognizable. The military belongs to "We the People" and as it is populated by Americans and not by blue helmet UN troops, it is a distinction that we suppose our military personnel are intimately aware of. We must assure that no institution that serves us be more committed to the spirit of the Constitution than our own military. However, we cannot pretend that even within our military there are not forces that have aligned with the enemies of the imperatives required by a strict adherence to the limitations imposed on government by the Constitution.

There is an interesting case that addresses an aspect of our military's responsibility to the spirit of the Constitution. Most people are unfamiliar with a Court decision from 1804, the case of Little v Barreme. It was known as the Flying Fish case. The Flying Fish was a Danish vessel seized by a Navy Captain in December 1799 pursuant to an order from President John Adams. The order was inconsistent with an act of Congress which declared that the government had no authorization to seize those vessels. The ship owners sued the captain for trespass in United States maritime court.

On appeal, Chief Justice Marshall rejected the captain's argument that he was only following the presidential orders and could not be sued. Marshall noted that the President's order, because of Congress's action, was not within his powers. Consequently the Court asserted that commanders "act at their own peril" when they obey wrongful orders.

Can it not be reasonably argued that orders by a President that are unconstitutional are obeyed by generals and other military personnel "at their own peril"? That the President himself executes those orders at his own risk and peril; that the President is the chief law enforcement officer, but that he is not above the law? The Flying Fish case also provides a Constitutional rationale for the military to stand as a bulwark against usurpation by the Commander in Chief of authority he does not lawfully possess.

Still, our military are trained to obey the civilian authority and as our Constitution dictates, they get their orders from the Commander in Chief. It is those whom we have entrusted to command them that we must monitor.

Results are the only measurable standard by which to evaluate effort. A nation that possesses the most powerful military in the history of humankind, yet finds itself in a continuous state of undeclared war for over sixty years, has failed miserably to be an example of the benefits of a policy of peaceful free trade, and has certainly failed to effectively use the deterrent powers of its military strength. This does not speak well of those to whom we have assigned the responsibility of directing our international relations, and to whom we have entrusted the treasure dearest to our hearts, our family members who have volunteered to serve in our armed forces.

Our public servants have failed in this regard for several reasons:

First, they have succumbed to a minimalist and petty vision.

Second, they have colluded with entities and persons whose interests are contrary to the well being of their overseers, the sovereign free men and women of America.

Third, they have disparaged the Founders' vision of a separatist foreign policy.

Fourth, they have disregarded their obligations under the Constitution.

Fifth, they have disrespected the Laws of Nature and Nature's God and acted as though their wisdom was superior to historically confirmed principles.

That our public servants in positions of authority, too many of whom scoff at the notion that they serve and "We the People" rule, would not hesitate to order our armed forces to point their weapons at the families of their fellow soldiers presents a terrible moral dilemma. It exists only because the beast has escaped its cage and is now in part under the control of tyrants. This is unacceptable and must be reversed.

Our public servants in government have betrayed us. That this may not be misunderstood or understated, it bears repeating. They have betrayed us. Because of this betrayal, our brethren who have volunteered to serve in our armed forces have suffered unnecessarily. This does not diminish their praiseworthy sacrifices, but it does condemn those who have arrogantly abused of the willingness of Americans to give their all for their ideals, their fellow man, and their country. We can change that, but first we must challenge ourselves to look deeply within, and confirm the righteousness of our own convictions. As we think things through, we must answer difficult but important questions.

For example, are we to conclude that liberty is dysfunctional because of the irrational negligence of those whom we have elected to serve us?

26 - Is Liberty Rational or Absurd?

"It is the greatest absurdity to suppose it in the power of one, or any number of men, at the entering into society, to renounce their essential natural rights, or the means of preserving those rights; when the grand end of civil government, from the very nature of its institution, is for the support, protection, and defense of those very rights; the principal of which, as is before observed, are Life, Liberty, and Property. If men, through fear, fraud, or mistake, should in terms renounce or give up any essential natural right, the eternal law of reason and the grand end of society would absolutely vacate such renunciation. The right to freedom being the gift of God Almighty, it is not in the power of man to alienate this gift and voluntarily become a slave."

Samuel Adams

"We are in the process of creating what deserves to be called the idiot culture. Not an idiot sub-culture, which every society has bubbling beneath the surface and which can provide harmless fun; but the culture itself. For the first time, the weird and the stupid and the coarse are becoming our cultural norm, even our cultural ideal."

Carl Bernstein, U.S. journalist. Guardian (London, June 3, 1992)

Let us acknowledge and consider why true liberty is rational. Genuine liberty does not authenticate its bona fides by applauding the absurd.

Let us consider some essentials of liberty as understood under the movement we call libertarianism. Libertarianism as a philosophy is not restricted to any particular political party, although in the last several decades as of this writing, it has not found measurable companionship in either of the major political parties.

Paul Phaneuf

Libertarianism is committed to the belief that men and women should be free to determine what is in their own best interest. Libertarians believe that freedom works. And generally, libertarians believe that most intrusions by government into the lives of adults are an imposition that is a violation of liberty.

Many people mistakenly believe it is inconsistent to be a conservative Christian and also a libertarian. This is not true. Let us explore concepts that hopefully will offer some insights that will be thought provoking. Perhaps after consideration, some Christians who did not think themselves libertarians may reconsider, and maybe some libertarians who could not imagine that they could accept Christianity will reevaluate their conclusions.

Like many other topics that we have considered, this one subject could become many books. Let us examine it within the context of individual sovereignty under God, the purpose of this book, and as it intertwines with our obligations to government.

Let me make some general observations. There are no "proofs" offered here. The impetus of your own deliberations must tweak your interest. You decide for yourself and where necessary, if you feel so compelled, do your own research.

First, libertarians are not anarchists. Libertarians are not opposed to the rule of law. Libertarians understand the need for government, but they are committed to limited government.

Strict social conservatives might consider some libertarian positions extreme. Libertarians generally oppose any laws criminalizing drug use. That does not imply that they advocate drug use. They might as individuals choose to be very involved with programs to help people to stop abusing drugs. They might personally donate time and money to charities and institutions that are very active in the championing of a drug free lifestyle, but they adamantly oppose the use of coercion by government as a tool.

Rational libertarians, however, would distinguish between illegal and unlawful. Many things which the government as nanny has made illegal, they have done by statutes that are, in fact, themselves a violation of fundamental laws of Nature because they disregard liberty.

Our Constitutional government is not authorized to impose itself in the private decisions of adults, yet it routinely does so. That is because the federal government is in the hands of elitists who think it is their job to run everybody's life.

There are really only two reasons why one adult would try to run another adult's life. The first is that they believe that they are so much wiser than you. You are such a dunderhead that they need to violate even the very Laws of God so that they can rescue you from yourself and the "horrifying" consequences when you act in a manner other than that which they have approved for you. They are the absolute worst kind of do-gooders. They are the busy bodies of the world who "tsk-tsk" you before they zap you with the cattle prod.

The other reason is that they have an agenda that is not about what they believe is good for you, but rather what is good for themselves. There is a very real global cadre of totalitarians who have used everything from Malthusian threats of global starvation, global cooling, global warming, climate change, unionism, Communism, Marxism, Statism, Fascism, and various other discredited "isms" to deceive and enslave billions of people. It is they who violate the Law. And they too have cattle prods.

Also, unfortunately, many people who genuinely seek to live honorable lives mistakenly equate legality with justice. They confuse the ideal, which is statutes that are true to the principles of Law, and fail to recognize the perversion that occurs when what is truly unlawful is given the color of legality. It is why America today has become all about legal plunder in the guise of good intentions.[57]

Libertarians as a rule believe that government coercion violates liberty. Now if for example a drug addict steals or harms another individual directly (as opposed to "mere" moral repulsion), a libertarian would generally consider the protection of property rights a legitimate function of government.

Rational libertarians do not advocate for or favor stupid choices or actions. They understand that in free societies, some people will choose to do inexplicably dumb things. They may even be committed activists who seek to persuade and help the poor and the needy, but as a rule, libertarians, of whom I am one, believe that property rights are sacrosanct. And there is no more immediate property than one's own body.

It is fair to ask how one reconciles the belief that there are some things that are clearly right and some things that are wrong, with the belief that people have the freedom to be wrong.

First, we must recognize that the right to be wrong and to engage in foolish self destructive behavior does not extend to harming others by direct action. It does not imply toleration of gross negligence that causes direct harm to others. Society has a right to expect an individual driving a car to act responsibly. Drunks have no business exposing innocent others to thousands of pounds of hurling metal in the control of a grossly impaired mind.

That is why the notion of the Laws of Nature and Nature's God is an admission of core principles that apply to life while limiting both government and certain kinds of destructive behavior. It is also why the Founders articulated that our system of government was unsuitable to any but a "moral" people.

The notion that liberty is not license can be complex in its application. We are frequently confronted with the consequences of the imperfection and limits of our understanding and our desire to strike an appropriate balance between freedom and responsible behavior. However, because it is difficult does not mean that we should not strive.

It is true that society as a whole is harmed when people make bad choices and do stupid things. Nevertheless it cannot be denied that history has proven beyond any reasonable doubt that governments that are given the power to allegedly protect people from harming themselves inevitably aggregate to themselves the power to stop people from being themselves.

History has demonstrated that within the realm of human activity, there is no source of pain and suffering among men that is greater than the pain and suffering those men inflict on one another through abusive government power. There is no escaping that reality.

When our hearts ache for some poor fool who has abused himself and paid a terrible price, even if society has paid a price too, in the end, the greater evil is the inevitable monstrosity that governments become, and the horrible price that abusive governments impose upon great masses of individuals. We are confronted in an imperfect world with the lesser of two evils: occasional abuse and its consequences by individuals of themselves or massive abuse of free people by governments.

Another line of thought suggests that some libertarians may be libertines. This conflicts with those conservatives who believe that license and liberty are different concepts. However, most conservatives who may also be Christians understand that theocracies are just a different type of potentially abusive government and prefer to persuade rather than coerce. Theocracies run by men, whether Christian, Islamic or any other religion are unacceptable to any libertarian, even a Christian libertarian.

An important distinction is that while the libertarian perspective is that the government should not intervene with a private decision, it does not mean that government should sanction or approve personal irresponsibility or behavior that is antithetical to the realities of the nature of our beings.

Truth be told, there are blurry lines in the debate. Some issues are regarded by conservatives as common sense and not religious; and pure libertarianism sees no place for government where some social conservatives might argue that the culture must be protected.

In a truly free society where liberty and not license are the objective; where life, liberty and the pursuit of happiness are the goals; families and voluntary institutions such as churches and community organizations will encourage standards and try to influence, whereas government would seek to prohibit by violent means. In an earlier time, when government here was less intrusive and not all pervasive, De

Tocqueville marveled that his observations of America confirmed this perspective.

More than once we have drawn the distinction between liberty and license and we have done so for a reason. The point was made often and well by the Founders, and also in the Judeo Christian Scriptures. The survival of liberty imposes an obligation on those who genuinely love freedom to actively encourage and seek to persuade members of society to restrain from public excess, and aspire to the highest and best from themselves and each other. There is ample room within this framework for individuality, personal tastes, and private preferences. Depending on one's view, each man answers to God, or fate, or destiny for his personal choices.

Nevertheless, we must never forget, and history demonstrates conclusively, that a society which devolves into licentiousness descends gradually into chaos. This eventually necessitates intervention by the government which we have formed, to enforce respect of our mutual rights. Responsibility to monitor and engage in the formation of the character of our culture is a serious one, because the consequence of neglecting that duty leads to the death of true liberty.

Still, in our efforts to influence, the distinction between coercion and persuasion must always be respected. Why? Because every dictum of government from the vital to the mundane is concluded with two usually unspoken but silently iterated words that carry the ultimate threat of death: "...or else..."

Obey, or else. Or else what? Or else restrained; or else incarcerated. One would resist these things? Then, or else shocked by tasers, or choked by gas, or bludgeoned, or even executed for resisting the escalating responses of government. The government is the threat or use of violence even when applied to the most commonplace activities of free men.

Is it not shocking that we today apply this escalating mechanism of violence to the tiniest infractions of regulatory statutes that are a not breach of True Law, but are rightful resistance to oppressive rules? Is it not the right of a man to say no when his rights are despoiled? Is it not his responsibility to resist this intrusion upon his God-given liberty? Is it not obvious that our obsession with regulation of minutiae is an infringement on the rights of men?

Is not the right of free men to voluntarily contract among themselves essentially, and of a profound nature, different than the use of government to regulate every tiny aspect of human activity using force?

Do we really want to stop other free men from doing what in our view is harmful to them by using the threat of killing them for their own good? Yet understand; that is what government is. That is what the use of force implies and entails. Government is always about "or else". That is why government is limited. Better persuasion than coercion.

I remember as a youngster growing up in the 1950s that there were no statutes that made unwed motherhood "illegal", but societal pressures discouraged women from having children out of wedlock. In a free but responsible society, families, institutions, and churches promote certain moral and ethical standards but, except to the extent that individuals voluntarily submit, they lack the power of coercion.

Again, it is true that the system is imperfect. In the end the relevant question is which system will tend to produce the greatest good; which system will cause the least harm?

Despite limitations and abuses, the system that accomplishes both of these results is freedom.

History clearly demonstrates that because it is the sanctioned use of coercion and accumulates power to itself, government always becomes the most vial abuser of people.

In my Christian paradigm, I reason that if God allowed me the liberty to accept or reject Him, to make consequential decisions to turn to Him or from Him, who am I to restrict the liberty of another?

This is not to say that there are no limits to freedom, as we have discussed. To tolerate is not necessarily to approve. To restrict the government's power to prohibit is not to tacitly promote. To restrain the government from restricting does not mean that society is required to encourage. To defer is not to sanction.

Edmund Burke wrote that all that is necessary for the triumph of evil is that good men do nothing. Let us remember that there are limitless opportunities to "do something" that do not require the compromise of liberty and resorting to unleashing the coercive intrusions of government contrary to the Laws of Nature and the limits imposed on government by our Constitution.

Freedom is tolerant but it does not need to sacrifice the rational. Liberty is required to tolerate foolishness; it is not required to celebrate the absurd. Liberty does not demand that we institutionalize the ridiculous. We can and should affect our culture by example and persuasion, but we as individuals should not resort to violence or coercion except in defense of innocents, or self, or family; or in defense of liberty, and then only as a last resort.

In considering the rational as opposed to the absurd, is it rational to ignore indisputable evidence when it is in plain sight? This is what is required if one would plead the case for government control of everyone and everything. Government is the use of force extended over every area of life that it touches. Clearly, the use of coercion under the color of law in opposition to true Law is the ultimate absurdity.

The question of government control leads to another question over a different aspect of life. Are socialism and free enterprise so complicated that only economists can decipher and comprehend them?

27 - Free Enterprise or Socialism?

"Agriculture, manufactures, commerce, and navigation, the four pillars of our prosperity, are the most thriving when left most free to individual enterprise."

Thomas Jefferson

"The enviable condition of the people of the United States is often too much ascribed to the physical advantages of their soil & climate .... But a just estimate of the happiness of our country will never overlook what belongs to the fertile activity of a free people and the benign influence of a responsible government."

James Madison

Winston Churchill is credited with having said that, "Capitalism's problem is the unequal distribution of wealth. But Socialism's problem is the equal distribution of misery."

The mechanism which drives free market activities is sublimely simple. Adam Smith offered the theory of an "invisible hand" that guided economic activity. He was using this as an illustration to describe what seemed to happen in a free market. This is in contrast to the iron fist that pummels a free people in a controlled economy.

Freedom, free enterprise, and capitalism function through a means whereby millions of free people, either individually or through the companies they form or invest in, make millions of economic decisions on a daily basis; what to do for a living, what to buy or not to buy, where to invest, what doctor to see, what insurance to purchase, whether or not to take a vacation; how much to save, etc.,

Paul Phaneuf

etc. Each of these decisions made by these free people are based on an assessment of reality and conducted by each individual, or group, or association in what they perceive to be their own best interest.

It is so simple. It is just free people and institutions each making what they hope and believe is the best possible move.

Sometimes they are right and sometimes wrong, but millions of times every day millions of people process small amounts of data and results are assessed and reassessed. Goals are reset, actions taken to adjust, and people take their profits and losses over and over again. When their decisions are correct, people take their gains; when they make a mistake, people accept the consequences and they make adjustments based on what they have learned.

Millions of decisions made by millions of free people pursuing their own best interests and ideas of happiness, based on millions of considerations of manageable amounts of data adjusted continuously on the basis of millions of evaluations. The efficiency of this model is actually beautiful to contemplate. It literally creates wealth. How?

Imagine vast numbers of entrepreneurs, looking to discover a need they can satisfy, to inspire a desire for a new idea or invention, or a better way of doing something, or a project they want to build, all the while hoping that people will freely choose to purchase their product, or pay for the service they provide, so they the entrepreneurs can care for their families and achieve their own dreams. Imagine these entrepreneurs restrained only by their need to do their best and be honest, unimpeded by moronic despots who think they have got everybody else's business figured out and who are willing to use coercion to force other people to do things their way because by some freak of nature, they are somehow the smartest creatures on the planet.

In a free market, a beneficial, commercial exchange of value happens when each party leaves the transaction satisfied that they have gotten what they wanted. And they did not even need Nanny with a cattle prod to tell them they had to do it for their own good. Is such a world possible? Surely not, say our masters in government. However, multiply these transactions by millions of times a day and lo and behold you find people growing wheat, who sell it to people who turn it into flour, who sell it to people who bake bread, who sell it to people who own grocery stores, who sell the bread to people who eat it. What a bizarre concept!

Coincidentally, this is the system by which we became the wealthiest nation on earth, a country with fewer people who do not have enough bread to eat than any country in the history of the world. This only happens efficiently in a free economy. Freedom is the grease that makes it flow and the glue that makes it an organic whole. Despite what Nanny would like you to believe (no offense to all the real nannies that do not ever use cattle prods), this is not a theory. Freedom as it is lived in the real world creates wealth. This is uncontested by honest people who are willing to look at history.

This is Smith's invisible hand that guides the economy of a free society and literally produces abundant wealth. When you unleash people's imaginations and energies in a values based free market, there are no limits in this abundant universe to how much wealth can be created. Now just for the record, this is a simplistic explanation of how the markets work. All kinds of insights and concepts come into play that increase one's expertise in the intricacies and mechanics of commerce, capitalism and free enterprise, but the principle behind it is not hard to understand.

For all the government people who might be reading this, here it is in two words: freedom works.

The American experiment confirmed the truth that liberty and limited government produce wealth, and the rest of the world has benefited from our prosperity and charity. Regrettably in 2008 we elected a President who felt a need to prostrate himself before the world apologizing for our success. Somehow we are supposed to be ashamed that the Laws of Prosperity were confirmed when our commitment to freedom procured for our nation the blessings of Liberty? We need not be ashamed of free enterprise, despite its challenges, but we should be embarrassed that we elected such a dangerous nincompoop.

A wealthier people mean more opportunity for entrepreneurs to creatively find ways to do and make things better. More wealth in the hands of a free people in a values based society means more jobs, better jobs, more pay, more progress, more inventions, more people looking to create "a better mousetrap"; more charity, more voluntary institutions to care for the needy, the dispossessed, and more resources available for families to care for their own.

The wild card is the insidious intrusion of government. Government violates individual freedom and imposes itself, inserts itself in the guise of such euphemisms as "incentives" or "tax breaks" (which are usually nothing more than government relinquishing that which it had no authority to take in the first place). Taxes, fees, and fines so imposed are part of the bureaucratic maze of obsessive controls through which the rats are supposed to steer. Those who "serve" intervene and construct obstacles along pathways which free men ought to have the right to navigate unimpeded.

This is not to impugn all taxes, or all fees, or to deny that there might actually be legitimate needs to allocate resources to facilitate (not micromanage) the commerce in which free men would engage. However, it is government that is restricted and limited by True Law and the Constitution, so all revenue proposals must be judged through the prism of the rights of property, and the necessity for policy choices that are the least intrusive upon the actions and choices of free men.

There is a subtle distinction of purpose. One is to look at tolls, or taxes, or fees as an occasional necessity to fund the legitimate but limited functions of government. The other is the use by wolves in sheep's clothing who, with the most endearing smile, seek in fact to channel the herd to enable the governments' pillaging hordes of official plunderers.

To be kind, let us say that at best they see themselves as the wise and benign overseers who believe that they are superior to the Laws of Liberty and must control the masses for their own good.

Those to whom we entrust power must be held to this standard: they are always to look at the tasks before them through the eyes of a servant, not through the eyes of a master. Public servants may not rule and they are never authorized to restrict our unalienable rights. It is culpable neglect when public servants fail to diligently seek the least invasive pathway to accomplish lawful ends. That is their duty.

Another false premise, that a free market society is less compassionate than a coercion society, is completely inane. They are opposite animals from the starting line. A simplistic analogy might be that the free market points the gun in the air to indicate the start of the race; the government has a gun pointed at the participants threatening to shoot them if they do not run according to some predetermined outcome.

Where does the government's legitimate role come in? Well, to start with it should not be pointing the gun at either of the race participants. It should be enforcing the notion that the race be run honestly and neither racer should be pointing a gun at the other. To be accurate, the government should not even be holding the starting pistol. That decision is made by the free market.

The government is the servant mechanism that enforces the agreements "We the People" freely enter into among ourselves and provides the civil opportunity to deal with fraud or any other dishonesty. It is not the government's role, or within its authority, to direct or micromanage or interfere with the property rights of sovereign adults, which includes decisions as to how they will apply their labor, except in extremely limited circumstances that are provided for in the Constitution.

Where statutes and rules are needed to promote trade and protect the unalienable rights of honest dealings among various people who may obviously at times disagree, they must be evaluated according to their conformity to honest contracts voluntarily entered into, the limits imposed upon government by the Constitution, and the common sense natural rights of sovereign individuals. This is one of the proper roles of government in its capacity to "govern" a society of free people and their free enterprise.

Creeping socialism is the economic disaster and the financial tyranny that begins to invade and compromise the free enterprise system at the moment legislative and bureaucratic pirates begin to interfere with the honest dealings of free people and their voluntary institutions.

The perversion of true capitalism, Crony Capitalism, occurs when counterfeit adherents of free markets and free enterprise, oftentimes large corporations that note the susceptibility of men in power to compromise for personal gain, insinuate themselves into the power structure of government, and seek to unlawfully use statutes and the color of law. Rather than compete honestly in the market-place they resort to the corrupt use of government coercion to gain advantage.

Crony capitalism is as insidious and destructive as pure socialism and is the equivalent of any other habit forming activity. They first indulge, acquiring a taste for the profits that come from using government to leverage statutes on their behalf. They taste the forbidden fruit, advantage gained by alliances with corrupt public servants, and they become addicted. They lose their edge and now will stop at nothing to get their fix rather than exercise the necessary energy to sustain their economic health. They too are plunderers and should be scorned. They are nothing more than uncommon thieves.

By way of contrast, under socialism and the central planning model, a small number of persons and institutions oversee vast amounts of data and make grand decisions based on assumptions, presumptions, and agendas. They then use coercion, whether through compulsion, threats, brute force, bribery, or trickery to force the people they have subjugated to follow the orders of those who rule over and dictate to them. Here arrogance, even hubris, crawls into the calculations. The self interests of those who sit in power infect their decisions.

This cannot be avoided, for the same limitations that contaminate the hearts of free men are found in the hearts of those who see themselves as superior to those over whom they believe they have a right to rule. Only now the damage is on a larger scale. The ultimate arbiter and judge of this methodology is history. Socialism has been tried and retried and does not work.

Good intentions are insufficient and cannot compensate for bad results. Again, socialism does not work. This is incontestable. Beware the motivations or mental capacities of those who refuse to acknowledge the incontrovertible historical evidence of socialism's failures.

In the light of indisputable results that discredit it, we must conclude that socialism and its malapropisms (progressivism, etc.) is a mental disorder because it ignores reality. This is a delusional malady of the mind and soul.

It is like a skin disease, a cancer that spreads a creeping crud. In order to stifle it we must be on the alert for the first signs of its infection, otherwise what might be easily uprooted becomes a wart with sinews that run deep into the flesh. The cure becomes a gaping flesh wound that is ugly, repulsive, takes a long time to heal, and may even leave a disfiguring scar.

Socialism is the mental meltdown of an entire society. It is the end of aspiration for those who are seduced into its promise of protocols that exchange groveling for a ration of the bare essentials of life. It develops a "settle for" mindset and shrinks the imagination of men.

Two additional important considerations to note about socialism: first, it interferes with the sovereign man's right to control, develop, or dispose of his property and thereby violates the constitutionally protected unalienable rights of man. It stymies innovation and warps the lens through which opportunity is visualized.

It arbitrarily obstructs the path of voluntary transactions which are the heart of free markets and free enterprise. These are grasping hands that grab and pull at the fabric that is the warp and weave of freedom, for it is the antithesis of liberty.

Woefully, there are always some who believe that while it could not be done by others, they bring some supposed magical calculus to the equation that has escaped lesser men. When you encounter this demigod, this messiah, zip your wallet, gather your children, circle your wagons and prepare for battle. Your freedom will be assaulted. Do not sleep without a lookout; do not repair the foundations without your sword at the ready. An attack is imminent.

Alternatively, where liberty is entrenched in a large community, as already noted, freedom allows millions to make informed decisions in their own best interests. Socialism and central planning are the means some men utilize to make themselves overlords through the use of force.

In every system, some men are corrupt or inept or incompetent. In every system, sometimes honest, well intentioned men are wrong and sometimes honest, well intentioned men are right. Only freedom and the free enterprise system allow each individual to at least attempt to direct his own destiny, to set his own goals, to make adjustments according to his own best judgment.

Do not fall for the false premise that freedom means every man for himself. Humans naturally congregate and form alliances. It is in our nature to be social. From the beginning we had families, clans, tribes, villages, towns, cities, states, nations. Under freedom, the alliances are voluntary. Under central planning, they are dictated.

The accusation that free enterprise and capitalism are "dog eats dog" individualism is propagandist nonsense. In a free society it is in the best interest of he who would succeed to provide both real and perceived value. Only this brings free men back to the table to purchase from the basket of goods that you offer. Shoddy service is shunned and a bad reputation leads to the demise of a business.

Fraud, deceit, and dishonesty are a violation of true Law and that is why we organize into governments so that the use of force may be wisely and uniformly applied, and only when absolutely necessary.

In a free society, adults do not form governments because we want our servant to be our master; or because we are orphaned and need nannies to wipe our runny noses, or demand that we put on overcoats because Nurse Nanny with the cattle prod thinks it is chilly outside, and we might catch a cold; or especially not to commandeer our liberty for our own good.

Understand and repeat this truth and do not remain silent when you hear it assaulted or discredited: Freedom works. Freedom works. Freedom works.

It is my hope that as we continue this discussion, whether you agree with everything you read in these pages or not, you will find yourself empowered and prepared to engage in the battle of ideas. Under no circumstances should these pages be the end of that exercise. Rather, may they add to what you have already acquired along your journey, or may they provide a starting point from which you may begin what must be a lifelong discipline for each of us. In the end we shall learn from one another as we have learned from so many others who have paved the way before us.

We are all travelers who walk a path that has been cleared by others. Let us follow them together.

That being said, should we not be wary of following the crowd blindly?

28 - Is Democracy Mob Rule?

"Remember democracy never lasts long. It soon wastes, exhausts, and murders itself. There never was a democracy yet that did not commit suicide. We are not a democracy."

John Adams

"The democracy will cease to exist when you take away from those who are willing to work and give to those who would not."

Thomas Jefferson

"Democracy is two wolves and a lamb voting on what to have for lunch. Liberty is a well-armed lamb contesting the vote!"

Benjamin Franklin

Let me reiterate the words from John Adams. "We are not a democracy". To foster the idea that we are a democracy is to plant the seeds of destruction for the Republic which our Founders created and the liberties which we sought to enshrine and protect under our Constitution.

It is a canard to pretend that the American experiment which produced the wealthiest nation on earth was a product of that which has cannibalized its constituents every time it has been tried in the history of humankind: pure democracy. Stop referring to our country as a democracy and start referring to it as what it is: a Republic.

The Founders' despised the notion of pure democracy. Essentially they believed that pure democracy was the equivalent of mob rule; that it was too easy to excite the passions of a mob, that a mob would readily take from

Paul Phaneuf

those who produce to satiate themselves, and that a representative form of government would allow reason, principle, and dialog to ultimately yield the best hope for rational and wise decisions.

They felt that demagogues used crises to the disadvantage of reasonable considerations and that history had demonstrated that pure democracies predictably self destructed. Clearly the lessons of history pointed to a Republic as that form of government which stood the best chance of survival and granted the greatest protection to the citizens of a nation. This is merely stating the fact, not making the case. To hear the arguments in detail, one should read Bastiat, or Cicero, or Locke, or read the Founders own writings, including the letters they exchanged for years after the founding of our Republic. The arguments are persuasive, in fact, irrefutable.

What exactly is a Republic and what kind of Republic did the Founders' give us? It is important that we understand the difference between a Republic and a Democracy. If we are uninformed we are destined to be manipulated by those who do know the difference. The evidence of this is the current tyrannical federal government, a gargantuan parasite that has invaded every orifice of our bodies and sought to control every aspect of our minds and spirits, even to the perversion of ordinary common sense, completely and utterly contrary to the limitations imposed by the Constitution.

A Republic is a representative form of government. It is a specific application of democracy that tempers the reactionary impulses of mobs. The people elect individuals to represent them in executing the government's mandate.

America is a specific kind of Republic. We are a Constitutional Republic. This means that those who represent us are limited in their power by the specific terms of the written social compact. Our country has two fundamental documents that are the equivalent of a mission statement and an operational charter. The mission statement is the Declaration of Independence and the operational charter is the Constitution.

Our Constitutional Republic is deliberately constructed and as is discussed in the next paragraph, through the Bill of Rights, is specifically construed to limit the power of the federal government to a very narrow range of activities.

In fact, the Founders were so concerned with the historical tendency of government to parasitical excess that they included an additional charter with its own preamble, the Bill of Rights. The preamble to the Bill of Rights, i.e., the first ten Amendments to the Constitution, states that the amendments were included to "prevent misconstruction or abuse of its [the federal government's] powers", and that "declaratory and restrictive" clauses should be added that would best "ensure the beneficent ends of its institution".[58]

While the preamble to the Constitution overviewed certain functions that would be the responsibility of the federal government, paramount was the notion that its purpose was to "secure the blessings of liberty to ourselves and our posterity."[59] The reader is encouraged once again to refer to the resources at the end of this book, specifically those that expand our understanding of how the Constitution was designed to accomplish this end.

Between the Declaration of Independence, its acknowledgement that governments could not abridge God-given rights and the pronouncement of the Constitution that its purpose was to secure the blessings of liberty, it is unambiguously clear that our social compact subsumes the Supreme Law of the Land to the Supreme Law of Nature and Nature's God. This God is recognized in the Declaration as our Creator. Anyone who feels that liberty is too confining will find no lack of countries that will accommodate their desire to be ruled rather than to be free. Here, one is free not to believe in that Creator. However, one is not free to be rid of those of us who do believe, or to limit our expression of that belief.

It is time for a revolution of the hearts, minds, and souls of America against the delusions of grandeur that the federal government has inserted into its infrastructure. The servant must be disciplined, reminded of its limited duties, stripped of its accumulated powers usurped from the people and the States, and rendered fit for its enumerated responsibilities.

The only violence this requires is the violence we the people must endure as we force ourselves to do what is required of us to retrieve our lawful freedoms; it is the violence of self discipline and it is not inflicted upon anyone, it is imposed by us upon ourselves. We have become a slothful people and our image is unkempt and devoid of legitimate pride because the anemic condition of our liberty reflects our laziness.

The bad news is we did it to ourselves: we let snakes slither into our liberty garden. The good news is we can root them out.

The question is what frame of mind is required to accomplish this end? Clearly we have not acted, as a people, in a way that has tempered the government's folly and unrestrained growth. Since thought precedes action, how must a free man think so that his actions will be consistent with his desire to impact his servant government and preserve his liberty?

PART THREE

MINDSET

"*Laws are made for men of ordinary understanding and should, therefore, be construed by the ordinary rules of common sense. Their meaning is not to be sought for in metaphysical subtleties which may make anything mean everything or nothing at pleasure.*"

Thomas Jefferson

"*I have little interest in streamlining government or in making it more efficient, for I mean to reduce its size. I do not undertake to promote welfare, for I propose to extend freedom. My aim is not to pass laws, but to repeal them. It is not to inaugurate new programs, but to cancel old ones that do violence to the Constitution, or that have failed in their purpose, or that impose on the people an unwarranted financial burden. I will not attempt to discover whether legislation is 'needed' before I have first determined whether it is constitutionally permissible. And if I should later be attacked for neglecting my constituents' 'interests,' I shall reply that I was informed their main interest is liberty and that in that cause I am doing the very best I can.*"

Barry Goldwater **THE CONSCIENCE OF A CONSERVATIVE**

29 - Stand Firm

"If ever the Time should come, when vain & aspiring Men shall possess the highest Seats in Government, our Country will stand in Need of its experienced Patriots to prevent its Ruin"
Samuel Adams

"Suppose you were an idiot. And suppose you were a member of congress. But I repeat myself."
Mark Twain

It is impossible to stand firm if you are not on solid ground. If your feet are not planted, you will be easily toppled. If you are constantly off balance because you have been pummeled repeatedly by the same blows, remind yourself that you are not a punching bag. It is OK to defend yourself. If you have to, hit back. On rare occasions, it may even be necessary to hit first. Regardless, it is time for a reassessment if you are finding yourself constantly on the ground.

The purpose of this book is to provoke thought. Forgive me if this appears condescending. Of course I cannot know each individual who reads my words. Perhaps you are someone who is versed in the paradigm of principle, familiar with the lessons of history, reasoned in your thinking, humbled by your own imperfections, aware that each of us has limitations, but ever striving, ever learning, ever open to improvement and truth as it is presented to you. Congratulations, you are a rare breed.

I say this not because I am superior. I have fallen many times in my life. I am in no position to throw stones. Of course, neither is anyone else, so do not bend over to pick up any rocks because you do not like what is said. I am humbled by my own mistakes but not blinded to yours. We all live in glass houses. We are not reaching for some unattainable perfection. It is about not allowing the unattainable best (perfection) to get in the way of the better (freedom).

My conclusion that too many people cannot answer questions like, "who are you," "what do you believe," and "why do you believe it," is based on the condition of our nation. If more people were not gliding through life on semi automatic, we would not have the intrusive government we have today. It is the old saw: the proof of the pudding is in the eating.

We are on the verge of national bankruptcy. For the last four years this nation has had a President who appoints Czars (Caesars) as casually as he would skip rocks on a pond, or more appropriately, slice a golf ball. And as of this update on November 7, 2012, he has been reelected by hordes of individuals who seem to have no regard for irrefutable facts and who seem more inclined to vote for celebrity than truth.

As a people we are burdened, suffocated by tens of thousands of pages, millions upon millions of statutes, rules and regulations that infest every aspect of every decision we make. In what parallel universe is this considered freedom?

Assuming you are still reading and you are one of those who think people like me are Chicken Little (not likely); forgive me, truly, if my words offend you. But the facts speak volumes, and your thumb sucking little nappy time is about to end whether you like it or not; or are you so naïve that you think this nation can become insolvent, a condition that will collapse the global economy, without disturbing your pleasant little reverie? While it is not becoming, I am begging. Please wake up and let me out of your nightmare.

If you are among the newborn that have awakened to the state of our national emergency, welcome to the real world. Get an education and do it quickly, but in the mean time, get active politically. You are reading this after the 2012 elections and the Obama administration has remained in power. The prior four years project an economic trajectory that is compelling and frightening. Get cracking. Drowning or not, we have to keep swimming.

As America still has a redistributionist Statist in the White House, we must seek another course. We must plan for the next election, but more importantly, we must reach out and educate. What level of ignorance, what depth of misunderstanding would motivate people to reelect a President with the worst economic record in modern times, a statist for whom freedom is nothing but rhetorical flourish?

What could possibly motivate Americans to allow a party to retain the Senate when that party has dishonored its own statutes, and failed to pass a budget in four years? We must examine the depths of fallacy that people have bought into, or overlooked, and make the awakening of the American people a priority. We want to reach everyone. But to win, we need only find 5% who are now blind but are willing to see. It can be done.

We are well aware that the names and the dates change, but the election cycles continue. Assuming we can avoid or survive the impending financial debacle, and most observers posit that if we continue the current administration's commitment to a radical progressive ideology, we may not;

without great personal sacrifice by Patriots prepared to work for the sake of our children we will lose our hunger for victory. If we are to survive as a genuinely free country the battle must go on. The strategy remains the same: a Constitutional Republic serving free men and women who are "Sovereign Under God", but the tactics must change.

Never does the need for free men to keep their public servants in line abate. If we elect honorable men and women to serve in government, it is our responsibility to hold them accountable, to see that they keep their promises, to hold their feet to the Constitutional fire. Regardless of who wins, our job as overseers of our public servants never ends. The government is never your friend. As Ronald Reagan once quipped, the most dangerous words a man can hear are, "I'm from the government and I'm here to help."

Standing firm means we never cede an inch to the forces that oppose liberty. Not one inch, not ever. Even as we struggle to regain what we have lost, even if we are eventually blessed with victory over the Statists, and find ourselves once again truly free, encroachment by those who would abuse power will exist until the end of days. We will have to stand firm always. Stand firm.

30 - Reach Out and Unite

"For true patriots to be silent is dangerous."
Samuel Adams

"The Constitution is not an instrument for the government to restrain the people; it is an instrument for the people to restrain the government -- lest it come to dominate our lives and interests."
Patrick Henry

"Therefore, since we have so great a cloud of witnesses surrounding us, let us also lay aside every encumbrance and the sin which so easily entangles us, and let us run with endurance the race that is set before us..."
Heb 12:1 (NASB)

We must each ask ourselves the question: are we in this fight to win it? Freedom is an all or nothing proposition. There will be no compromise of liberty, no deals, no promises in lieu of real change in the direction of government, no struggle for its own sake, no symbolic sacrifices without expectation of substantive progress, no acceptable result other than victory. We need to work with those who are committed to winning. We must unite with like minded sovereign people.

And let me distinguish something for myopic tyrant wannabes. This is not about the "Sovereign Citizen" movement. This is about a plane of existence that transcends sovereign citizenship. We are all citizens. To an extent, citizens are "governed". In our nation, we have clearly defined what "governed" means and of equal importance, what it does not mean. There is disagreement on the fringes but at the core, ours is in theory a limited government. It is not in fact a limited government as I write this, but it is supposed to be.

Citizenship is that status that speaks to our affiliation with some political entity, be it local government, state government, federal government, etc. As citizens of a city, state, and nation, we share a common bond. We share a compact, an institutional camaraderie, a sophisticated tribal alliance.

No, as I have already indicated, the sovereignty of which I have spoken throughout this manuscript refers to our status in the order of our being. However, as it applies to this practical application in our lives as Americans, I want to clarify it in anticipation of the distortions that will be proffered by those who are opponents of liberty and the restrictions that the concept of unalienable rights imposes on government.

Advocates of government as some be-all-end-all answer to every problem in life will attempt to characterize my positions as "dangerous". I understand why. Truth is a disinfectant and it destroys distortions and lies. Truth is dangerous to fantasy disguised as reality. Truth is the enemy of tyranny. But truth is not dangerous to you and me. That is an important distinction.

As a Christian, my first citizenship is in heaven. I am here as an ambassador with dual citizenship. My first loyalty is with my primary home and that is with God. Naturally, not all citizens of the United States share that understanding, and I respect that. I mention it because it is my status as a created being that brings to the forefront of my mind the awareness that while all men are created equal, not all beings are equal. There are categories and orders. God is superior to humans. Conscious beings are superior to unconscious things. The creator is superior to his creation.

As we recognized earlier, the government is a product. There is no society without individuals. Society is a result of the fact that numerous individuals gather together. Government is a created thing. It has no life of its own. It owes its very existence to the fact that superior beings to it exist and inhabit and rule the earth.

Government is a dumb tool. It speaks only through the voice of living, breathing human beings. It has no intrinsic merit or power of its own. Even the greatness of our own country is a consequence of the noble sentiments of living men that have breathed the essence of freedom into its construct and thereby inured to themselves the blessings of liberty.

I am not concerned with the comparatively trivial consideration of whether or not I am a sovereign citizen. In fact, I readily proclaim that I am not a sovereign citizen. I am a citizen in the kingdom of the King of kings, Almighty God, and am subject to Him. But I am a sovereign BEING under God.

In the Christian paradigm, it is the creature that rebelled against the Creator. Scripture says that one third of the angels rebelled and followed Satan. It tells us that Adam and Eve rebelled in Eden. You do not have to accept that. Again, it is who I am, not who you have to be. But surely you must admit to this: it is impossible for the Creator to rebel against the creature. This is a logical absurdity. It is the creature that rebels against the creator.

In our considerations let me emphatically articulate this position. It is the creature, what was supposed to be limited government that has over time been commandeered by unscrupulous men that has rebelled against the men who created it; men who are sovereign beings under God. One of the tactics that we must recognize, identify, and expose is the tactic of demonizing anyone who sees government as the problem. Those of us who suggest that there are solutions to problems that do not require coercion are not evil, and I urge that we not stand silent when confronted with this irrelevant tactic.

Let us also be conscious of the tendency to personalize government, to give it the status of a living thing. It is not a living being, and we cannot allow it to be so construed. Corporations in commercial courts are considered "persons". If that is true, then a living, breathing free man is a category of being that is superior to the legal construction of "person".

No rational human being will argue this point. He who lives and breathes and thinks; they who have formed government are transcendentally superior to it and to the legal constructs that subservient entities devise. If you cannot stand on this reality, you have no hope in defending your liberty in the long run. You are completely unaware of who you are. You will be conquered by your ignorance and will have to submit to whatever entity claims mastery over you.

Reaching out implies seeking out like minded individuals. How can you recognize the company of men who know who they are if you do not know who you are? How can you point to truth if you have not identified it in your own life? How can you know the difference between visceral reaction and thoughtful positions if you do not examine your own mind? How can any of us do this without the benefit of principled truth that absolutely exists independent of our recognition of it?

We must reach out, we must recruit; we must teach our children; we must unite if we are to take back control of our destiny and put the chain back on the beast of government. See the resources at the end of this book to find people in the freedom movement. Not all individuals will have thought all things through. None of us have. Perhaps it will be you who will spark a discussion that will provoke thought in the next President of the United States? If not you, who?

One final thought regarding this subject. We should be proud to be Americans. I have no interest in seeking out people who hate our country. Like you, I love this country. I hate what some people are trying to do with our country, and I despise what has been done to our government and what is being done to us by our government. But it is we who carry the torch of freedom. It is America that has been founded on the principle of unalienable rights from our Creator. We have much to be proud of. The desire to make things right is a sign of the love we have for our nation, one nation under God.

Find people who love God, love His creation, love our fellow man, love freedom, and love our country and seek and promote truth with them. We want a return to liberty not a revolution. The violent revolution that secured freedom in this country is commemorated on July 4th every year. That was violence enough. By the hand of Providence, we won the Revolutionary War; by the grace of God our nation survived the Civil War. What we genuinely want is a return to basics, a return to freedom, not more shed blood.

That being said, should we not enthusiastically resist tyranny?

31 - Resist

"Congress has not unlimited powers to provide for the general welfare but only those specifically enumerated."

"The greatest [calamity] which could befall [us would be] submission to a government of unlimited powers."

"When injustice becomes law, resistance becomes duty."

Thomas Jefferson

While I want to speak primarily to principles and the need for critical thinking, it is impossible not to address the real time events in which we are immersed as I write these thoughts. I would hope that if you are reading this ten or fifty years from now, you can look back and see that the slide into the overt tyranny of collectivism has been reversed.

Collectivism can be summarized in part as the notion that the group, as an institution, is superior to the individuals that comprise it. Again, we are social beings and our interdependency begins with the most basic group of all: the family. Let us never forget that no societal unit exists if there are not at least two individuals who form it. It is the human being that is real. Everything that flows out of our humanity is a type of construct, something we fashion. It is the individual man or woman that has intrinsic value; that is directly created by God; that has unalienable rights.

To anyone reading these words in the years to come, let the context of my words contribute to the resolve that we will never let freedom come this close to extinction again.

Paul Phaneuf

The battle for freedom is one to which each generation must commit and recommit. It never ends.

If you have had enough of the arrogance and presumptiveness of government, pass this book on to everyone you know; if it is too strong for your stomach, save it. If we do not successfully reverse our direction, it is only a matter of time before you consider my words tame compared to the abuse you will endure from your so called public servants; and that is only if you are not among those of us who already struggle to keep down our food every time we attempt to navigate the ways of freedom. We find ourselves up against another artificial barrier in the governments' labyrinthine schemes to micromanage our lives at every turn.

Why worry about being polite with elected officials? It is true that common courtesy is something we owe any individual. However, in the light of the trouble and imminent danger we face as a nation directly because of these same people, this obsequious curtseying to people with a title or position in government is sickening. While there are exceptions, and we have seen new faces that are resolved to restore the Founding principles, as a whole, overwhelmingly, our so called public servants are out of control and have long passed deserving respect or civility.

They lust for power and the praise of men and have long behaved not like public servants but rather like muggers, pimps, and prostitutes. If you were introduced to Jack the Ripper, would you call him "sir" when you discovered he was of "noble" birth? It is time to stop playing polite games. These arrogant swindlers have their hands in our pockets, their eyes in our private affairs, their thugs in our faces, and their knives twisting in our backs.

"Another bowl of porridge, please, sir?"

Americans Patriots don't bow before any throne but God's.

Let your elected officials know where you stand. Let them know you will not give up your freedom without a fight. Make it a political fight preferably, but a fight to the finish if necessary. Praise God for the Second Amendment. Thomas Jefferson had it right, and those who can turn a blind eye to the lessons of history and choose not to see the consequences of trusting government have it dead wrong. Government is not a trustworthy institution and is far too dangerous and powerful to be given free rein to abuse our individual liberties.

If you want to find the Constitution in Washington, D.C., these days, you have to look for little four inch squares of paper placed in toilets stalls throughout the Capitol. It is understandable. Washington, D.C. is a cesspool full of self serving sellouts who think we are simpletons.

Maybe your own elected officials are among those irresponsible buffoons who inexplicably voted for the largest spending bill in the history of the world without reading it? Given the lessons of history, how come only our elected public servants seem to have failed to see this coming? Warnings have been shouted from rooftops for decades. Or worse, they saw it coming and lacked the fortitude to address the problem.

Are your elected public servants among those who rammed government run healthcare down our throats contrary to a vociferous public outcry against it? If this 2,700 page jigsaw puzzle of lobbyists' back room deals, phony numbers, oppressive bureaucracy, and radical government intrusion into the healthcare decisions of a free people is such an advantage, why has Congress exempted itself from this legislation? How dare they? What hubris! Does this not offend you? They have authorized confiscation, punishment, controls for you, but they have placed themselves above this tyrannical law. Sadly, this arrogant behavior is routine.

Now that Obama has been reelected, this gluttonous power grab by government has little to prevent its implementation. Our task has just become more difficult, the sacrifice required of us to recover liberty greater than ever. It does not change the insight acquired into the Statist's mindset revealed in the following paragraphs:

Is it not shocking to recall that Nancy Pelosi, the Speaker of the House at the time, stood in front of the nation and informed us that we needed to "pass the health care bill to see what was in it"? That she was elected Speaker of the House by her peers demonstrates how systemic that thinking has to be among our public servants in Congress. It would appear that they do not accept that the word servant applies to them.

Take that mindset exhibited by then Speaker Pelosi and apply it to anything in life, and the massive absurdity of it speaks to just how great is her contempt of the people she serves. And she is one of many in government who think like this:

You have to buy this house to see what's in it.

You have to buy this car before you can test drive it.

You have to marry this man or this woman before you can meet them.

This is principled representation? No, this is the Speaker of the House telling you that she thinks you are an ignoramus. You are just too dumb to know what you want, and you need caretakers laying a safe path for you to run on in life. Thank God for all-knowing super humans that can protect us from ourselves.

Does it matter on what side of the political spectrum you stand? Do any of us want that kind of arrogance controlling our lives? These are so called public servants who refer to those people who have honestly attained success as being overpaid, but who have voted themselves lifetime perks. Their retirement packages are worth millions and they have done nothing but destroy our nation and interfere with our freedoms.

If we look at our own leaders and see rebellious hirelings, why would we think that international madmen out to exploit our weaknesses would not see the same obnoxious foolishness that insults our intelligence day by day? They see the American people reelecting devious, disrespectful liars time after time.

They see our President apologizing to the world because we are not perfect, as though the rest of the world has a record that is pristine. Does it not make you just a little sick to realize that we are the ones who keep sending these swindlers back to their cushy D.C. temples of duplicity and treachery?

Are you not getting tired of sitting on your hands while these jokers (in D.C., or even your own Statehouse) ignore you, figuratively spit in your face, and desecrate everything you hold sacred and holy? In the halls of power, principle is a commodity that is for sale.

Are you among the financially wealthy? If not, what do you have to leave your children and grandchildren besides faith and freedom? Have you not noticed? Both are under assault by the very people we have elected to serve us. They think their job is to rule...to reign...to control...to confiscate...to pollute our children's minds...to murder the unborn...to LORD IT OVER US.

To them, you are an ignorant peasant, a serf chained to the pig trough they have constructed and permit you to wallow in. You are a flea infested little rat in the maze of rules and regulations, and fees and taxes, and cultural experimentation and pathetic pseudo science that they force you to navigate at the point of government guns.

Unelected bureaucrats shut down fertile valleys, extensive expanses of productive farmland in California, depriving families of a way of life they had known for generations. Under what standard and from what source can they find the legitimate authority to deprive the rest of us from the literal fruits of these family farmers' labors and private property because of some supposedly endangered fish? The lunacy is beyond digestion.

We are led by a President who thinks that we should be punished for leading the world, through freedom and innovation, into an era of prosperity. We are evil because we achieved the greatest good for the greatest number, because our system based on freedom and free enterprise worked so well.

We need to apologize because we consume a larger proportion of energy, forgetting that we have protected and defended the world from hideous fiends, fed the world, shared with the world, fought for freedom around the world, were first in charity, first in progress, first in prosperity, first in liberty. This is from a President who inhibits and opposes utilizing our own natural resources but allows foreign nations access to those very things he has unconstitutionally denied the American people.

Is America perfect? No. And too often we have been lead down a destructive path by our public servants. Yet as the rest of the world seeks to emulate our success, for four years as of this writing we have been led by a man who bows before kings and grovels before antagonists.

I apologize to the world right now. I am so sorry that we elected a Marxist as President, a political Luddite, a man with a medieval vision, a man who has no understanding of economics, a man who lies, a man who capitulates, a man who lacks wisdom, a consumer of evil mental dribble that has been repudiated by experience and history. I am sorry, world.

And you, you silly stupid American citizen, how dare you think you have the right to make decisions for yourself and your family without the permission of your superiors? Just who do you think you are, a free man? You brazen little peon, you belong to the world. You are the property of the government. The world is sovereign. America is hateful. You are nothing.

Really, America, just how long do you intend to take this abuse?

This is not a time for violence, but it is a time for action. If you do not act, your children and grandchildren will curse you for allowing greedy, ignorant people to violate common sense, long standing hallowed traditions, and reverence for the Creator from whom our freedoms come. Do you want our generation to be the one that allowed freedom to die? Well it is happening right now, right before your eyes. Wake up. Talk it up. Vote the stinking bums out. But do not replace them with different bums. We have national elections every two years. Be resolved to make the next election cycle count. Every two years we get a chance to make things right. As a people, we simply have not tried hard enough.

Demand that those we elect to serve at every level of government acknowledge that it is not their job to set the course. This is the function of each individual. Government does not pave the way. It protects the way we the free people have paved. Government is not fit to lead. It is a tool. And it is responsive to free men or to tyrants. It cannot serve both simultaneously. There is no middle ground. If this is true of individuals because it is inherent to their nature[60] it is true of a collection of individuals.

Understand and internalize liberty's attributes. Informed patriots will respond quickly. Government intrusion into places it does not belong can be curtailed before long term harm is inflicted on "We the People". In a Constitutional Republic, free people lead and government, through the elected public servants we hire, follows. It is a dance. It is not complicated, but it is subtle.

"We the People" lead, not as a mob, but as reasoned men committed to principles through elected representatives. This does not mean that elected representatives cannot initiate. Of course they must. We do it through them. What it does mean is that the will of the people to be free must be so deeply embedded in our national paradigm that even those we elect to serve us are themselves compelled to act only in the interests of liberty. And when they deviate from that, they do not get a redo in the next cycle. They are retired.

We lead by virtue of our unconditional commitment to freedom's cause, by our diligence, and by our urgent response to those who would enslave us by removing them using the most proximate lawful means: remonstrance immediately, impeachment if necessary, and voting them out at the earliest possible electoral opportunity.

Resisting is not enough. How can we press forward?

32 - Press Forward

"It is the duty of the patriot to protect his country from its government."

Thomas Paine

"Today, we need a nation of Minutemen, who are not only prepared to take arms, but citizens who regard the preservation of freedom as the basic purpose of their daily lives, and who are willing to consciously work and sacrifice for that freedom."

John F. Kennedy

One might ask why I look at resisting and pressing forward as two different objectives.

I see resistance as reactive. The government moves to intrude, to insinuate itself into another part of our lives and like the boxer, we parry the blow. We resist government by determining not to allow it entry to where it was previously barred or absent but where it now seeks to gain another foothold. As it seeks to advance, we move to stop it.

There are numerous people and organizations that have great resources, determination, and skills to execute resistance. Seek them out and join. Resources are included at the end of the book. Email me if you know of an effective organization that should be included. This list is not complete and needs your help. It is important to realize that the commitment to press forward must be done on the individual level in concert with others.

To press forward is proactive. As government continuously encroaches upon liberty, it is incumbent upon us to press the envelope and expand the territory that is already ours. Similarly we reach into the monster's lair and retake territory that is rightfully ours. Like a bloated water bag responding to gravity, government imposes itself where it has no business going.

In every case the best exposure is the light of day. The process has already begun. Ordinary citizens are now attending public meetings of local officials that have always been open but have been consistently ignored. Government has operated with impunity. The very presence of the eyes of the people restrains the actions of government on every level. It only takes a few people who commit to watching to completely pull back the curtain and expose what is now happening unimpeded under the cover of citizen apathy.

Every publicly open meeting should be attended by ordinary citizens (even just one!) who monitor with the intention of informing and exposing what government is doing in the people's name. At one time the media took this responsibility upon themselves, but we as a people are fools to entrust this to anyone but ourselves. And not astonishingly, few meetings among public servants have any reason to be held in secret. Secret meetings by public servants should be treated like an advance warning of coming abuse.

Pressing forward is maintaining pressure against an object that is the equivalent of gravity or magnetism. It is never ending, unrelenting, and entirely predictable. Like water, government power at every level seeps into every open crack or crevice. Power hates a vacuum. Our choice is press forward or be overwhelmed and consumed.

Are resisting and pressing forward morally right? Let us think that through.

33 - Retake the Moral High Ground

"A better system of education for the common people might pre-serve them long from such artificial inequalities as are prejudicial to society, by confounding the natural distinctions of right and wrong, virtue and vice."

John Adams

"...Virtue, morality, and religion. This is the armor, my friend, and this alone that renders us invincible. These are the tactics we should study. If we lose these, we are conquered, fallen indeed...so long as our manners and principles remain sound, there is no danger."

Patrick Henry

True Liberty IS the moral high ground and it is time that we assert our standing. This was a self evident truth for the Founders. The moment an argument deviates into the moral relativism of coercion (violence) in the name of anything other than the defense of individual freedom, that person and that argument have ceded the moral high ground. This is the first clue that manipulation and compromise of unalienable rights is in process.

STOP! Do not accept the underlying premise that is being presented to you by those who argue the need to violate individual freedom. Coercion by government that is not in defense of liberty is an assault on that liberty. Do not be tricked into arguing about the gnat of good intentions while you swallow the camel of tyranny.

Beware this red herring, a favorite of moral relativists. It is an attempt to pivot, to redirect, to put a defender of freedom on the defense. It is generally framed in some form of the following bromide: "if you are not in favor of... (my big government solution), then you must be in favor of the problem."

The error, even the deliberate mischaracterization, is the incorrect premise that you do not acknowledge some problem or other; that you do not care. This becomes the acorn of justification that manifests as political correctness that then grows into the oak tree of hatred. To see its outworking in the extreme, look at what the Nazis did to the Jews.

The unspoken moral conclusion is that you and your freedom-oriented, non-big government, non-coercive solutions are therefore evil. How can you not want government to "do something about it"? The lie is that there is only one way to fix the problem. The pitfall is that people have been indoctrinated to look to the government first.

In most cases the government should not be looked to at all. Of course no freedom based solutions are found if no one looks for them, or if they are never tried, or the government does not allow them to be considered. This is common sense, yet it is ignored, as though looking first for solutions that do not compromise liberty is not fundamentally necessary to develop and retain a free society.

The danger is that people see liberty as negotiable, and as Benjamin Franklin once said,

"Those who would give up essential liberty to purchase a little temporary safety deserve neither liberty nor safety."

The simple fact is no system is perfect; all systems have holes. Jesus Himself said that there would always be poor people among us that we can help.[61] It is a distinction with terrible consequences if we get it wrong. To choose to resolve problems within the societal infrastructure and support that develops in an environment of freedom is infinitely preferable to the feeble, abusive results that consistently and predictably occur in an environment of oppression.

It is deliberate folly to ignore the obvious truth that government is the least productive, least efficient, most ineffective, most expensive, most corrupt, most harmful, and given our Constitution and the Free and Sovereign nature of Man, completely unlawful way of solving 99% of all the problems it currently handles. Looking to government as the first resort rather than the last is the antithesis of the moral high ground. It is the moral gutter.

There are legitimate functions for our limited government but the Founders made clear that, in their view, government is at best a necessary evil. Like handling nitro glycerin, it leaves little room for error. It is immensely useful in its proper place. It is highly destructive when misused.

The new paradigm of the government as provider of all things necessary weakens the building blocks of a society. Free, creative people grounded in right principles constitute the raw materials that make for a liberty based culture. Government as nanny diminishes free people and only feeds those who advocate for more government power. Government power does not exist independent of two elements: those who rule and those who are ruled.

In some instances, as in the common defense, as in the facilitation of trade among the states, as in the arbiter of last resort in the civil courts, as in the establishment of statutes that require honest dealings in commerce, as in the enforcer of true law against interstate brigands and thieves, as in presenting the face of "We the People" to the world; all of these, and others so enumerated, are legitimate functions of the federal government, but they are narrowly defined and absolutely limited by the unalienable rights of the people that it serves.

There is no moral equivalence that justifies the servant dictating to the master. For those who wonder how government could possibly do what it needs to do in genuine states of emergency, the answer is simple. In a truly free society, real emergencies will see ample volunteers who will respond and rise to the occasion. We see that aspect of the American character, the human element of compassion even in today's restrictive environment. Imagine its strength and capability when people are not bound, pillaged and restricted by an overbearing government. That is the moral high ground.

When talking about "emergencies", we are not talking about the never ending contrived crises that exist because government has overreached in the first place, and that government uses as a justification to tighten the noose it has placed around our necks. These are the kind of crises that initiated this remark from President Barack Obama's Chief of Staff: *You never let a serious crisis go to waste. And what I mean by that it's an opportunity to do things you think you could not do before.* In one context, this could be interpreted as an opportunity to test one's resolve and willingness to overcome adversity. In the context of an executive branch that appointed 40 Czars (what Constitution?) and has consistently expanded an already bloated government, the statement is absolutely chilling.

We are talking about genuine emergencies. These are the events that cannot be prevented, like acts of nature or accidents. Might there be some legitimate need to coordinate some disaster through the Federal Government? This question would succumb to a reasonable argument if we did not have a culture that phrased every government intrusion into the lives and Liberty of free people as some kind of "war;" a War on Poverty; a War on Drugs; a War on Smoking. If war is the arbiter of that which justifies extreme government actions, then wretchedness shall be the permanent condition of Liberty, as there shall be no arena in which limited government may be demanded by the people. This is precisely where we find ourselves in these times, except that it may now be said that our government is in a permanent state of war against freedom.

Surely it can be argued that even wars between nations would be minimized if we had a non-interventionist foreign policy and we maintained our peace through strength and trade. Despite our shortcomings, the world has recognized our charitable nature. Americans are the first to respond in every calamity. Why would that aspect of who and what we are diminish in the fruitful soil and prosperity of real liberty? The answer is it would not.

One of the challenges is that we have lost the ability to imagine and visualize how a value based free society could actually function in the real world. We have been living in this fake freedom for so long that we think we actually need the crutch of government in our daily lives. We have been conditioned to believe that we have a bad leg so we have stopped trying to run. We think first in terms of government solutions (read: liberty restricting, coercion based), and fail to seek answers that are compatible with our values.

We see what we have been told to see. Like the man who gets on his hands and knees to find the tiny screw that he has dropped, and his mind focuses and dismisses anything that is not that screw, we no longer see possibilities that don't resemble government remedies. It is a most pitiable myopia. We become victims of a horrifying vicious spiral into tyranny, because if it is tolerated, the government will always predictably metastasize into a parasitic controlling freak of nature. When an otherwise free people allow that to happen, they have chosen the path of least resistance. Again, this is not taking the moral high ground.

Internationally, as Jefferson articulated, let us have free trade and friendship with all, entangling alliances with none. It is not an isolationist foreign policy but a separatist policy that the Founders envisioned. With those that behave as friends, we interrelate, we trade with them, and we support them. Those nations that do not behave as friends, for them we limit access, we watch them like hawks; we stand ever prepared to offer genuine friendship, but the world knows that we stand ever prepared to defend our sovereignty, our lives, our property and our way of life.

We have the capacity to produce ever increasing, in fact virtually unlimited wealth through the development of our own energy resources and the liberation of American entrepreneurs from the restrictions of a bureaucracy run amuck. We welcome interdependency with all nations in this day of global communication and travel but we must depend on self reliance and American independence and hegemony for our basic needs and existence. To do less is moral neglect and virtual treason.

Individuals sovereign under God in free societies, developing free institutions, functioning in free markets in a value based culture will meet the most needs of the most people in the best way. This is the lesson of history. This is the moral high ground. It is only denied by those who have ulterior motives or are blind to evidence. We are fools if we do not proclaim the wisdom of Nature and Nature's God and the experience of the Founders from the highest moral planes. The moral high ground is ours, and we are less than men (i.e., free people) not to take it and hold it.

The ultimate conclusion is that we must act, but right action follows right thinking. What else do we need to mentally internalize in order to do more than just hang on, but thrive?

34 - Hold Fast

"If Congress can do whatever in their discretion can be done by money, and will promote the General Welfare, the Government is no longer a limited one, possessing enumerated powers, but an indefinite one, subject to particular exceptions."

James Madison

"Hold on, my friends, to the Constitution and to the Republic for which it stands. Miracles do not cluster, and what has happened once in 6000 years, may not happen again. Hold on to the Constitution, for if the American Constitution should fail, there will be anarchy throughout the world."

Daniel Webster

We are the problem. For decades we have let politicians act like lords and barons treating us like serfs. We have been gullible fools and behaved like trusting children, and let the make believe magician convince us that the thumb showing between his fingers is actually our nose.

We have sold our liberty and allowed usurpers to compromise our Constitutional protection in exchange for trinkets and baubles that are mostly empty promises intended to appeal to our worst impulses.

We are expected to believe that our free market institutions cannot radically impact our destiny as a nation; that our fate is beyond our control; that only more government can save us.

In 2012, at the time of this writing, we find ourselves dependent on nations that despise us primarily because our current chief executive has exceeded his legitimate authority and sabotaged the people's ability to insure our own survival. He has consistently obstructed access to the resources that sit under our federally controlled land and exist in abundance offshore. The blame is shared by a complicit Congress whose negligence is evidenced by a Senate that has failed to pass a budget for four years contrary to its own laws.

We are standing with one foot off the edge of a 900 foot cliff, the only thing that might save us is a skill we may not have, base jumping, and we have a parachute but we will not put it on. Why? Because a man many of us would not follow out of a burning building tells us we can't wear it because he said so. Instead we argue the equivalent of whether or not we should open an umbrella to break our fall.

I blame myself. I remember the last oil "crisis". In the late 70's I bought land, guns, and butter and like a fool thought the conservatives had awakened when we elected Ronald Reagan. I thought George H. W. Bush was his kinsman. After all, he was the Gipper's VP. And like a cowboy with a toothache I bought the snake oil and "read his lips".

Next, America elected an obvious egocentric con man named William Jefferson Clinton. While a man of few scruples who appears to have read Machiavelli, he was a pragmatist who was capable of putting his finger into the air and following the wind.

Are you old enough to remember the Time magazine cover years ago that warned of global cooling? Decades later many of us watched astounded as Al Gore got rich getting a new generation to work itself into an irrational frenzy over global warming. Since true science makes a case for neither, slick egocentric operators simply change the language: now we are supposed to panic about "climate change".

It's clever when you think about it. Absolutely dishonest, or course, but that is irrelevant in the world of parasitic power mongers. After all, when does weather not change? When do weather patterns not vacillate over time? Nature itself is the scary monster that only more government can manage. The manipulators of the masses press the panic button at will. Facts are irrelevant. Everything is an emergency that justifies more government to solve invented problems with the tools of oppression.

I voted for George W. Bush because he was a Christian and there is much about him that I wanted to love, but I fear, despite his best intentions, he nursed an affinity for globalism that was in his daddy's genes. He is right, though. Besides God, it is history that will be the judge of the decisions he made.

I too waited with baited breath while the drama of vote manipulation played itself out in the 2000 presidential elections. So many Americans are unaware that this was hardly a new phenomenon historically, despite the fact that we Americans prefer an idyllic sensibility about the sanctity of our votes, as we should.

And then from the mighty oak dropped the little acorn and voter fraud was born again. From it sprang the ultimate nightmare: a deceived people elected a man steeped in Marxist ideology named Barack Hussein Obama. The American people fawningly anointed him with the mantle of living the dream of Martin Luther King, Jr.; that dream a noble one, but forlornly we draped it around the shoulders of a progressive whose life had been constructed around the notion that the Constitution was a flawed vision; that

America was primarily a colonialist aggressor; that there was nothing unique about our halting attempts to create a nation and culture based on the notion that all men are created equal and endowed by their Creator with unalienable rights.

We put him in the White House, and as of this writing, he is the man who stands in the way of the recovery of our nation. He is not its savior; he is its destroyer because his ideas are inimical to individual liberty.

As of November 7, 2012, it became apparent that the task before us is even greater than we had imagined. Barack Hussein Obama, he who called upon his supporters to vote out of revenge, whose record is one of immense failure and expansion of the statist regime, was reelected by a razor thin margin. Apparently the American people have not suffered enough. Sadly, under Obama, they will.

We however must remember that we have been blessed with a Republic in which we can remonstrate, assemble, influence, reach out, educate, revitalize, invigorate, and resuscitate the American spirit of freedom, overcoming and accomplishment.

Our pressure on politicians must be relentless. We are at the precipice. We are not too late, I trust, but we are about to step off the cliff and we are holding the umbrella, not the parachute.

This movement must accelerate its sense of urgency. The umbrella will not cut it to break the fall. If we do not don the parachute, we are finished. As of 2012 we must deal with this job-killing, liberty-destroying health care blunder, and tackle the task of energy independence. We must rein in the bureaucrats, and ignite the engines of free enterprise. And we need to responsibly harvest our own abundant natural resources.

Amazingly, all we have to do is get the Feds to do what they do best: next to nothing. Let that failed leader run, panting to catch up to a freed American vision, waving his arms while he blubbers "Stop them, I'm their leader. Which way did they go?"

We must recover the American dream with a renewed sense of urgency. We must hold fast to the dreams that freedom liberates in the hearts and minds of men. We are about to enter uncharted waters, waters that can only be safely traveled if we navigate steadily focused on the pole star of freedom, that gift from God that we must hold inviolable and onto which we must tolerate no breach. We must hold fast in the storm which approaches. It will require courage. I believe that grounded in principle, we can be equal to the task.

We must ask a probing question and answer it honestly: is it possible to hold fast to what we have and value if we sleep and fail to post a watch to warn us when aggressors assault the stronghold of liberty?

35 - Eternal Vigilance

"There are more instances of the abridgment of the freedom of the people by gradual and silent encroachments of those in power than by violent and sudden usurpations."

James Madison

"Remember, my fellow-citizens, that eternal vigilance by the people is the price of liberty, and that you must pay the price if you wish to secure the blessings. It behooves you, therefore, to be watchful in your States as well as in the Federal Government".

Andrew Jackson, Farewell Address, 1837

Eternal means never ending. It implies that freedom is never guaranteed. It is claimed, protected, and defended or it is gone. That is the lesson of history. Vigilance requires a state of alertness. It is the act of watching for possible dangers.

I would like to suggest that the kind of vigilance we need is best demonstrated by several illustrations.

The Wallendas are a family of high wire acrobats. In 2012 one of them crossed Niagara Falls on a tightrope. With every step he took, he was vigilant. If he were not, he would surely have fallen. He lost his grandfather in an accidental fall during a performance many years ago. For just a moment, someone was not vigilant.

If you work with rattle snakes or cobras, you are vigilant. If you are not, you are poisoned.

If you work with alligators you are vigilant. If you are not, you will be bitten, eaten, or drowned.

Paul Phaneuf

If you work with explosives, defuse bombs, you are vigilant. If you are not, you are dead.

If you were a Roman sentry and you were found to be less than vigilant, you were executed.

If you are a free man and you are not vigilant, you will soon be in chains.

Freedom as we have seen is fragile. It is constantly under assault. It is not just governments. Too often one man is more than willing to sacrifice the freedom of another for his own gain. In our quest for eternal vigilance, we confront the very nature of man. We must be vigilant because the first danger to freedom lies within each one of us. It is self interest that is not contained by self restraint. It is complacency and apathy.

I've never run a marathon, but once you get into your sixties you realize life is one. This is the nature of the ongoing battle to regain and then retain freedom.

A friend of mine ran the Boston marathon years ago. He trained for months and he had one goal. Finish it. He had no illusions of coming in first or setting any course record. He wanted to achieve a personal objective, enter and complete the Boston marathon. He described to me how toward the end of the race every step was a decision to endure. Every cell in his body screamed stop. No more. To what end? Why bother? Why torture yourself?

One step after another, in pain, the end so close he could reach out and tickle it with his fingertips, yet each step seemed almost unattainable. Of course, this would not be much of a story if he was not successful. He was. He has reveled in that moment when he crossed the finish line for years. He takes out the photo and glows as he remembers the pain and the days it took him to recover physically, and the sense of peace and satisfaction he felt because he did not give up. It is this commitment of heart, mind, and body that is required to be vigilant in the cause of liberty.

Today's political climate has seen the growth of many movements, gatherings of people committed to reclaiming our heritage. From the Tea Party to groups formed around the Bill of Rights; freedom of religion and expression and the First Amendment; the right of self defense, to keep and bear arms, the last resort against tyranny, the Second Amendment; the limitations on the federal government, State's sovereignty, powers reserved to the people, the Tenth Amendment. Even the Seventeenth amendment that deals with how Senators are elected is being reconsidered.

These movements are both a cause and an effect. They are an effect because they are the response of a newly awakened free people to oppression. They are a cause because they become catalysts for outreach and constructive change. For decades the American people slept, comforted by the abundance of freedom's blessings and the historically indefensible delusion that freedom was a given in America. Clearly, it is not.

Consider the consequences when you start to get tired, when you see your neighbor growing weary, when every step is an agonizing recommitment to your values and the future of your children and your country; when it hurts to wake up and see another betrayal by your public servants, another state legislator running like a mouse from his oath of office, another politician compromising, another public sector union thug misrepresenting the rank and file and assaulting opponents, another indicator that we are shoveling against the tide; remember that the next time you fall asleep and fail to be eternally vigilant, you may wake up in chains that not even your grandchildren will be able to shed.

We have committed to a marathon for the highest and best reasons, against all odds, despite setbacks, through discouragement, betrayal, and bone tired weariness because we are right. Our cause is just and necessary. Neither you nor I need to get there first; we just need to finish the race. One more step; again, again, again. This is the nature of eternal vigilance. It is not a day trip, it's a life commitment and if we don't pass a sense of urgency about it to our children, their children will wake up slaves.

Please do not minimize the use of the word slaves. Bondage, serfdom takes many forms. As I write this the average American works for the government until sometime in May. Every dollar that we sweat to earn is confiscated in an orgy of taxation: federal and state income taxes, unemployment taxes, use taxes, sales taxes, social security taxes, payroll taxes, excise taxes, inheritance taxes, inventory taxes, luxury taxes, Medicare taxes, property taxes, capital gains taxes, licenses, tolls, fees, permits, penalties. Think about it.

For almost six months out of every year we pay everything we earn to the government. Is it no wonder that the dole seems so attractive? We surrender liberty and opportunity for bare subsistence and substitute shallow self gratification for substantive progress.

In the mean time, we are rewarded for allowing the government to house break us like puppies - how wonderful, we no longer pee on the carpet - and we get our daily bowl of dog food and a pat on the head. What kind of selfish rebels would ask for anything more from our masters? Why, that would make us potential terrorists!

Don't your children and grandchildren, your posterity and mine deserve better than that? Are we really willing to give them less than our best and our all so that they might live free?

36 - Freedom and Our Children

"A diffusion of knowledge is the only guardian of true liberty."
James Madison 1825

We cannot leave to our children what we do not have. If we have squandered our liberty through indolence and neglect, it is not only we who will pay. It will be a burden borne by generations to come. As Patrick Henry noted, that which has happened once in 6,000 years is not likely to happen again.

This book has been about the mindset that I believe is necessary to defend liberty. It is uncompromising and in many instances I have been deliberately hyperbolic. I make no apologies for any excesses that I have made in my effort. If I could figure a way to do more within the framework I have chosen, I would. As Barry Goldwater once said, "Extremism in defense of liberty is no vice."

It is those who would pass laws that must make their case, who must justify their actions. It is not the free man who must explain his liberty to those who would restrict him from activities that are lawful under God. My focus has been to empower my fellow sovereign beings with thoughts that contribute to the defense of liberty. I may have fallen short, and I am regrettably aware that in many ways it is inevitable that I have because I am just an ordinary man and this is an extraordinary challenge.

The real question is not can you defend freedom, because of course you can. I say this not because you have managed to make it thus far with me, but rather because liberty is a true, just, and noble cause and it is eminently defendable and the cause is worthy of the effort. The question is will you?

Will you teach others to think this through as you have? Can you see that it is not that we must travel the same road to come to liberty but rather that we must have the same end in mind? You have not lived my life. I have not lived yours, yet we both seek freedom. It has been stolen from us. We must take it back.

However, even more disquieting is that the methods used by those who have sought to enslave us have been directed to a long term end, and in order to achieve that end, the perpetrators of this evil have stolen the minds of our children. And this is the reason that only my commitment to God restrains me in this battle. Those who would assault our children with their various "isms", those who would compromise parental rights and responsibility; any entity which would place itself above the claims of righteous parents or between them and their children, between parents who do their best in difficult circumstances, that creature, that creation is a beast that cannot be underestimated and is deserving of vitriol.

From every quarter, from the books they read in school, to the programs they watch on television; from the music they listen to and the electronic games they play, the same message is drummed into our children's heads from morning until night.

It is the message of humanism, the worship of self; the subjugation of free men by big government; the portrayal of climate change as a manmade eco-monster; the presentation of the theory of evolution as though proven by unassailable evidence. They are being taught that government is the beneficent provider of all things good, that nature is a goddess, that they are citizens of the world, that America and the existence of sovereign nations is an obstruction to global peace and harmony.

They are being taught lies about God, about the Founders and the Constitution and the very nature of freedom, or they are taught nothing at all. They are being groomed to be a generation of sheep.

And who is behind this mysterious force that needs to mold our children into their image? It is a movement, a paradigm, a false narrative, a crippling mindset, an empty spirituality in the guise of planetary wellness and empty liberation from truth.

It is, depending on how you see things, the inexplicable unraveling of society, or the work of pernicious cabals, or the prophesied manifestation of the consequences of creation's rebellion and God's own resolution of the problem of good and evil. In any event, I cannot envision that it is the duty of free men to do less than resist evil and proclaim truth.

We must take our children back. We must teach them how to think. We must teach them the history of the servitude of men and the miracle of the American experiment. We must teach them the truth, to know our God. They must be informed about the good, the bad, and the ugly of the human experience, and we must empower them with the hope that our traditions and values, based as they on freedoms that are a gift from God can provide a course that is worthy of us.

We must teach them about liberty and we must teach them to teach their children, and we must resolve never to let the government have them again. This book is not the venue for specifics in this aspect of the battle, but hopefully within these pages you have found food for thought and principles worth teaching. Mine is one tiny effort at outreach in a flood of resources that are the product of the grand reawakening of the American dream. God willing, we are not too late.

God has His own plans for us all. As I see the world, nothing we do can thwart the will of God, but to the extent that He has placed our fate in our hands, to that extent we are obligated to expend an effort. We are in any event accountable for what we could have done but neglected to do. And since we cannot know the minute or the hour of His intentions, then we must stand in the freedom He has given us and try.

We must proceed as though victory is achievable because if we do not, we are already defeated, and our children deserve better than that. Please assist in this endeavor and contribute to the resources available currently at the back of this book, and also on the website at Sovereign Under God.

At this conjunction, events will unfold and forces unleashed by the "isms" of history will manifest. We may not be in total control, but we are not helpless pawns. We can make a difference. We can know that we did all we could to battle lies and the evil entities that tell them and that would sacrifice our children to their schemes. Regardless of destiny's final call, or as I see it God's consummate will, if we commit to teaching our children the truth, the truth will be sufficient and it will set us free.[62]

37 - Wrap It All Together

"I now make it my earnest prayer, that God would have you, and the State over which you preside, in his holy protection, that he would incline the hearts of the Citizens to cultivate a spirit of subordination and obedience to Government, to entertain a brotherly affection and love for one another, for their fellow Citizens of the United States at large, and particularly for their brethren who have served in the Field, and finally, that he would most graciously be pleased to dispose us all, to do Justice, to love mercy, and to demean ourselves with that Charity, humility and pacific temper of mind, which were the Characteristics of the Divine Author of our blessed Religion, and without an humble imitation of whose example in these things, we can never hope to be a happy Nation."

George Washington (circular letter of farewell to the army, June 8, 1783)

It is a humbling task for a simple man, a very ordinary man like me who has made mistakes, to consider lofty thoughts that I could only have fathomed by standing on the shoulders of giants like the Founders, and free market economists, and Philosophers who have struggled to apply noble principles to daily life. I have been blessed to stand on the pages of the Bible, what I have come to believe is the very Word of God. And I have been privileged to be lifted up by a simple man with an eighth grade education who chased his dreams, walked with honor, and led by example, my own father.

My father had successes and failures but in his final days as he lay on his death bed he assessed his life with these words: "I'm just a lowly man who did my best." Would that we may each prepare to meet our maker with a

Paul Phaneuf

sense of humility and the ability to accept that we ran our race, we did our best. More than any other truth, this lies at the heart of the reason we find ourselves as a nation staring disaster in the face. It is not so much that we should have done more. It is that we have too often, too many of us, not done our best.

Like most people I have found myself confronting my own human nature and the internal struggle of living up to what I know to be true. Sometimes reacting with anger is simply the way we would like to go because venting offers a type of relief. The effective patriot must cultivate a paradoxical and counterintuitive mindset.

It is not about blaming ourselves, it is about empowerment. The area of maximum effectiveness in the universe I inhabit is the attitudes and thoughts I allow in my own mind. If I change me, if I draw that line in the sand and take a stand, I change the whole world. I am powerless to enforce change in others, but I am mighty if I am willing to persuade with example and forthright and effective communication.

We change the world one person, one mind at a time, and the easiest place to start is with ourselves. This is not irrelevant psychobabble; it is the real world in practice.

As we become better informed, we have more to share. As we practice tolerance, not of the victim doormat variety, but in a gentle teacher mode, we influence. We do not compel. As the old saying goes, a mind changed against its will is of the same opinion still.

The goal is to help others have that "Ah-Ha" experience. We are enablers in the sense that we want to see the smile that reflects the dawning of the light of truth. This does not happen with a bludgeon. It happens when you realize that in possessing the truth, you have the cookie and if you offer it properly, in the end, eventually, everybody wants the cookie. You must not try force feed it to someone. You offer it. If he or she is not ready: NEXT! You have better things to do than to toss the cookie into the wind.

Passion is a must, but if we forget that beauty is in the eye of the beholder, we fail to notice when our passion is received as anger or nagging and rather than an open mind, our approach causes others to raise their defenses. Likewise, we need to accept that there are many who are entrenched in their views. Do not waste your time. Find someone who is hungry.

Obviously, as conservatives we believe that liberals are standing in quicksand, their wagons are hauling emotional baggage, their minds are darkened by a plethora of baseless opinions disengaged from fact, and if they are among the elite, they alone can claim to be a member of the rare and pure among us who can get up from the morning throne and swear to the presence of the fragrance of lilacs as they lift their trousers.

But the ordinary run of the mill liberal is usually a misinformed but well intentioned and otherwise decent human being who just happens to be wrong. Since the mind expanding awareness of the pathologies of public servants who prevaricate without remorse has crept into the consciousness of the voting public, many people have internalized a sense of unease.

No one likes to be wrong. None of us part easily with our cherished beliefs, but most of us will keep one eye open to find the door that leads to a new comfort zone if our foundations are shaken.

Make no mistake about it. The liberal next door is probably one of the many sleeping Americans who have simply surrendered unwittingly to the programming of the Progressive elites and their liberal media cohorts. In the right circumstances, free from peer pressure, if offered the cookie and not the stick, they will sneak a nibble.

Think about it, a mind starved of truth, swallowing mental swill from the pigsty of collectivism. How can they not be hungry? How long can you eat poison and not get an upset stomach? Set it up, watch for the smile because that nibble of the truth cookie tastes good. It satisfies.

I start with me. You start with you. We find someone hungry. We share a delicacy with them: truth, served on a platter of resolute determination, garnished with kindness, tempered with understanding. After all who among us has not overslept or pressed the snooze button more than once? We are not talking phony Pollyanna pleasant here, but you cannot make someone both an ally and an enemy.

Bring them along. Offer them reading, websites, social media. I have met many individuals who carry copies of the Constitution and readers with copies of important American documents. My brother gives people copies of Bastiat's **THE LAW** (an absolute must read!). Give someone a copy of this book.

Be sensitive to people's capacities and try to share compelling information and insights in palatable doses, being wary of the fact that people are unique and may respond differently to the same information.

Stay away from the deep edged fringe when you talk to someone you want to win to liberty's cause, even if you are convinced that you have uncovered the ultimate truth, because the uninitiated will not relate to you and will not be able to overcome their suspicion that you are a fruitcake and are a danger to the world as they perceive it. Their eyes will glaze over, they will internally shut you down, and they will back away.

And for the record, if you tell me you do not care about that, then you are a jaded fool, and your attitude is a liability to the cause of freedom, not an asset. Arrogance plays into our adversaries' hands.

Stick to core values and principles based on truth and on our country's Founding documents. Remember always that you are a sovereign man or woman under God, subject to His laws, a citizen of a nation whose founding values makes it the greatest nation in the history of the human race, and assuming you are a fellow American, so too may be the person you are talking to, even if they disagree with what you say.

Offer something really radical: patience and non judgmental friendship. It is the first step to becoming an effective Patriot. Do not expect to be applauded by the ruling elite. You will be vilified by them, but one on one you will find the occasional open mind, the person who has been questioning the disconnect between the lies government tells and the truth that imposes itself before their very eyes.

You do it one person at a time. You do it day after day. You teach and encourage others to do the same. Steadfastly, you move on to the next. Now you are changing the world.

Afterword

"The more laws, the less justice..."

Marcus Tullius Cicero (De Officiis, 44 B.C.)

"The state is the great fictitious entity by which everyone seeks to live at the expense of everyone else."

Frederic Bastiat (The State, 1848)

The time for complacency has not come and gone. That time never was. Every minute that we reclined, foolishly believing that the lessons of history did not apply to us will now exact a toll that we must pay to once again be a truly free people.

In fact, the toll will be exacted with interest. This is the price we pay for ignoring the warnings of the Founders, for allowing ourselves to give lip service to values and principles, for trusting fiends, liars, and monsters who actually believe that they are superior to the masses of humanity. Do not be deceived: their superiority is purchased. When they lie on their deathbed they will soon be entering into the next world naked like the rest of us, many of them whimpering and groveling as they crawl to their eternal fate. Their elitist corpses will putrefy and even the monuments to their own memories will erode and disappear. Their superiority is a short lived delusion.

For those among us who have remained vigilant and diligent there is the comfort of knowing that men and women across the land are enjoined to the task before us. Life, liberty and the pursuit of happiness, while unalienable

Paul Phaneuf

rights, are no longer seen as guaranteed simply because others have paid the price for us to enjoy them. The price must be paid to keep them.

For those among us who have slept too long but are now awake, we gratefully join hands and ranks and lean into the hard, cold winds of reality and move forward.

To those who are still asleep, we can only shout and call and wave and hope. Everybody is needed. We are at that station where the weight that must be moved needs every able bodied individual, and if yours is the muscle or mind that would have made the difference, you will live in chains with the rest of us regretting your indolence.

To those who do not care or will not see, we pity you.

To those of you who are public servants, if your hearts are true and you honor the sovereign station of your fellow man, you accept the limits of government and the authenticity of True Law, we thank you for your service and salute you.

A word of warning, however, regarding political parties: unfortunately the Republicans and Democrats have become the equivalent of Tweedle-Dumb and Tweedle-Dumber.

Let us not be naïve. Our choice is not A or B, Left or Right, Democrat or Republican. Our choice is Freedom or Bondage. We can leave the specific strategies and tactics to some other time or book, however let me state in no uncertain terms that to my mind, both parties have been overtaken by globalists and Progressives and neither can be blindly trusted. We must trust our principles and values and measure every politician individually against those standards.

Should we survive the financial conflagration, the spark for which our immolation has already been ignited; should we manage to manipulate the meltdown clock sufficiently to buy ourselves time, our only recourse is to run with urgency to replace the compromisers and liars from whatever Party with Patriots who are committed to limited, Constitutional government that leaves their masters, Sovereign People under God, free to live our lives according to our conscience.

Our battle may be enjoined but it is hardly won. Do not be deceived. If we would be free, no generation must ever again mindlessly recline in a self-induced stupor that leaves liberty to fend for itself.

To those of you who have no respect for our liberty, who think yourselves our masters, your time is over. We will warn our children and our children's children about you and we will teach them to do the same. We are Americans. And we are coming for you. To our contempt, history will add its record of your heinous crimes as well as its disdain. We bid you good riddance.

Any permission you thought you had to impose your will upon us in opposition to our God given liberties is hereby withdrawn. We are free and Sovereign Under God and we intend to live as free men.

What Is the Meaning of the Book's Cover?

The book's title speaks to our status as human beings in the real world as it is defined by our established place in the universe. This is an awfully broad subject, but, to my mind, our status as free and living beings, our position in the natural and supernatural order, and our relationship to government are as integrated as inhaling is to exhaling.

The cover is symbolic of the new relationship that exists between Americans and government at every level. Men with twisted minds have used government to advance themselves at the expense of their fellow man and have inverted the natural order. The worst offender is the federal government. But the paradigm of abuse which it has adopted bleeds to every level of government. Government, which is the servant that occupies the bottom rung, has placed itself at the top of the pyramid, above man and above God.

The upside down flag is not intended to show any disrespect but is, in fact, a universal symbol of distress. I love our flag because of what it stands for, regardless of how an elite cabal of usurpers has perverted our nation. We are a nation in distress; hence the flag is upside down on the cover.

The crumbling foundation is an obvious reference to our cultural, spiritual, financial and political condition. No edifice can remain standing on an unstable foundation. The foundations must be restored, or we will go the way of every nation in history that was blind to truth or lacked the determination, vision, courage, or fundamental values to do

Paul Phaneuf

what was required to repair the structural underpinnings upon which it stands.

A Personal Note

"My philosophy, in essence, is the concept of man as a heroic be-ing, with his own happiness as the moral purpose of his life, with productive achievement as his noblest activity, and reason as his only absolute."

*Ayn Rand (Appendix to **ATLAS SHRUGGED**)*

"For God so loved the world that he gave his only begotten Son, that whosoever believeth in him should not perish, but have everlasting life."

John 3:16 (KJV)

I implore your indulgence for one more thought. This is personal. I would like to share it with you if you will allow me to speak to my own spiritual faith and to essentially digress from the philosophical considerations, the historical context, and the political pragmatism which I have sought to present through this treatise. If a discussion of the basis of my own faith would offend you, I invite you to stop reading.

Otherwise, with your permission, here is a spiritual message I hope you will consider:

As freedom is a gift from God that government is not authorized to infringe as it is unalienable, there is another gift which I would like to share with you. It speaks to the essence of what it means to be a Christian.

Most people who are unfamiliar with the true nature of Christianity assume it to be a list of do's and don'ts which are primarily designed to take the fun out of life, put there

Paul Phaneuf

by a cranky old curmudgeon who basically doesn't have anything better to do than turn us into a bunch of boring, judgmental hypocrites. As was inescapably obvious in this discourse, I do believe there are some basic rules to living which God has given us that speak to our relationship with Him.

These might be controversial for someone who, for example, is a professed atheist or who is committed to an extreme application of Jefferson's reference in a letter to the Danbury Baptist Church about a wall of separation between church and state, a phrase not found in the Constitution, and which I believe has been perverted to twist the protection of freedom of religion into a freedom from religion.

Freedom from religion can only be achieved by suppressing freedom of religion and it is a dangerous perversion that makes religious expression a de facto infringement on the rights of those who prefer the religion of humanism to religions that worship God. Do not be deceived. Men who worship their own thinking, to the exclusion of the very possibility of a God who exists outside the natural realm, are practicing the religion of self.

The very presence of religious expression in the public sector is interpreted by them as an assault on their right not to believe, an intrusion into their universe where God is not allowed to exist even in the supernatural realm which they disavow. Is it not strange that they insist that we should not have access to what they have declared does not exist? It is an inherently self contradictory position, but such is their insecurity that in their minds, our faith affronts their disbelief and their faith in self.

Leaving that perspective aside for the moment, from a practical standpoint most of these rules which spring from the Judeo Christian value system (the "commandments") address the practical outworking of peaceful social interaction.

On a day to day basis, these rules are important. Many atheists would correctly argue that most of these rules for peaceful living among men may be deduced from reason and the observation of the Laws of Nature.

It seems obvious that these behavioral guidelines speak to some level of common sense and what some have called enlightened self interest. As such we frequently meet people who assert they are not people of religious faith but who nevertheless are genuinely nice people, productive, successful, and generous. After all, if there is any point that I have sought to make in these pages it is that truth exists, and much of it is discernible and discoverable simply by observing nature. This is why I quoted Ayn Rand at the beginning of these personal notes.

However, we are told in the Scriptures that there are some things about God which He has revealed that are special in that they could not otherwise be deduced unless God had told us forthrightly Himself. These are referred to as mysteries because by their nature they would not lend themselves to discovery. As for years we did not have the ability to explore the bottom of the ocean or walk the surface of the moon, so too does our finite mind lack the capacity to plunge into the depths of all things infinite.

If God is perfect and we are not; if He is infinite and we are finite, then despite how we might appear to be when compared to each other, the probability, even the possibility that we might meet His standards of perfection in the totality of our being are absolutely zero.

Contrary to popular belief, the meaning of the word "sin" is not restricted exclusively to actions which might be regarded as overtly disobedient to God, but rather its meaning in the original Greek is "missing the mark". In more than any other way, it is in this sense that given God's perfection and our obvious imperfections, all men "miss the mark".

If God's perfect standards demand truth and we have ever lied, doesn't that make us liars? Jesus said that if we have hate in our hearts that according to God's standards, we have murdered. Have you ever hated anyone? (You don't need to make a list.)

Jesus said that if we lust in our hearts, we have committed adultery. Have you ever lusted? (Let's not step into that one like Jimmy Carter did. No comment.)

If you have ever stolen anything, anything at all, wouldn't that make you a thief? (Just admit it. You're not the only one.)

If we went before an earthly judge because we had committed a serious crime; killed a man or raped someone, if we stood before the judge and said "Gosh, I'm sorry (I got caught)", wouldn't we still owe our debt to society, to the victim? Would we not be punished and go to jail?

While we can relate to horrible crimes against other people, we commonly struggle to imagine the serious nature of violating the dignity of an infinite and just God, spitting in His face and ignoring His commands, or just having the attitude that we all have at one time or another: "I don't care; I'm doing it my way".

If I hit my neighbor, he may do nothing. If I strike a police officer, I will go to jail. If I kill a Senator, I will probably never see the light of day and might even face execution.

What do we deserve when we violate the highest Being in the entire universe? Would our debt not be infinite? In fact God told the first humans that the penalty of sin was death. Physical death we understand, but spiritual death is eternal separation from God. He who is perfect cannot compromise His Just and Righteous nature and tolerate sin in His presence. An unrepentant debtor would pollute God's dwelling place.

Imagine standing before a judge in court. You have committed a major violation of some statute and the penalty is one hundred thousand dollars. You have nothing. A complete stranger walks in and offers to pay your debt. You accept the gift, the judge decrees that the debt is paid and you walk out a free man.

Here is the mystery and the miracle. In fact, we are merely finite creatures and we cannot pay a debt of infinite magnitude. What God has disclosed is that before He ever created free beings, Angelic and then Humankind, He knew that his creation would abuse their freedom. The infestation of sin into His universe did not take God by surprise. He chose to create free beings despite the cost to Him because He had no interest in the eternal company of robots who could not choose to love Him. Of course the ability to choose to love cannot exist without the ability to choose not to love.

The complete nature of God is beyond our capacity to comprehend, but God has revealed in Scripture that before time began, before He created anything outside of Himself, God's Son (this is a mystery) who is co-equal and co-eternal with the Father, volunteered to pay the price to settle man's debt to God.

God has disclosed that though He is a God of Justice, He is also a God of Love. So He, through His Son, became human and paid each person's debt.[63] Jesus died for me. He died for you. Jesus was innocent of any crime but assumed the curse of the cross of crucifixion and suffered and died as a substitute in our place.[64]

God resurrected Jesus from the dead in an act of Divine Love and has promised to do the same for us if we simply accept the gift of Christ's payment for our sins. Through Christ our debt is paid and we have eternal life merely by acknowledging that we are sinners who "miss the mark" and accept the gift because we realize we are indebted beyond our ability to pay.

This is what God has done for us. Eternal life cannot be earned.[65] It is simply outside our capacity to pay our debt to God ourselves and it is futile and arrogant to think otherwise. Christ paid it. He was God incarnate, sinless, and as such His assets, His ability to pay are also infinite. If we believe in Him and that He was raised from the dead so that we might accept His gift and be with Him forever, we are escorted into heaven when we die.

All you have to do is ask. "Lord, I don't fully understand, but I know I'm not perfect and I can never rise to meet your infinitely wise and perfect standards, but I am sorry. Please forgive me. I accept your offer for clemency, your gift of forgiveness, through the death and resurrection of Jesus."

God has promised that if you will offer this kind of prayer from your heart, humbly understanding your place before the God of the universe, He will forgive and save you and send His own Holy Spirit into your heart.[66] Instead of being spiritually dead and condemned because of your sin, you will be forgiven, redeemed (your debt paid) and reborn spiritually. It is faith in the promise of the same God who made you free to begin with.

If you would like to know more or have questions, please contact a local, Bible believing Christian church. Email me if you need help.

Don't look for perfection among we who are professed Christians. Not surprisingly, you won't find it. Hopefully this will save you from needless disappointment. We don't deserve the gift we've received anymore than anybody else. We will not know perfection until we die and join Christ in heaven. We still stumble and fall but we believe God and with His help, lift each other up. Someone will do the same for you.

Thank you for allowing me the privilege of sharing this important aspect of my faith with you and allowing me to go off topic; and thank you for taking the time to read it through.

It is what it is. Everybody dies. Living free in this life doesn't end up being worth all that much if we haven't opened our eyes to eternity.

God Bless and Live Free

Resources

I do not pretend that this list is, nor have I attempted to make it all inclusive. This is a mere taste of the resources available for individuals who would like to become involved, educated, resist, or unite with likeminded people, and who would like to restore the American dream of a civilization based on limited government, sound money, individual liberty and personal responsibility.

I'm leaving out so many great contemporary authors, from whom I have gained immeasurably, that I feel like I'm cheating you; among them, Glen Beck, Robert Bork, Mark Levin, Andrew Napolitano, Larry Reed, and John Stossel. In mentioning these few I am painfully aware of how many I have left out, but at least here you have a place to start. If you don't need a place to start, you probably already have many of the resources listed below and others. I haven't even touched great biographies of the Founders, which I personally love to read.

I've left out some of the classics like Cicero, Locke and von Mises because you'll be led to these and other great authors as you expose yourself to other books, web sites and especially informed people that you will meet in your activist journey.

Many of these sites have links to other organizations and resources. If you feel overwhelmed, find something about which you are passionate and dig in, dig deeper, get involved and make a difference.

Paul Phaneuf

Nothing here will be radical enough or pure enough for some; for others, some of these books, websites and organizations will be a dramatic leap into the unknown. This book is about you thinking for yourself. Make your own assessments and decisions.

This country is worth saving. Ignorance and apathy are tyranny's best friends. Be wary of pessimists (as opposed to realists who may occasionally sound pessimistic), skeptics, scoffers, statists, and liberals, all of whom will do nothing but discourage you and warp your thinking.

Please follow me on Twitter: @PaulPhaneuf

Facebook.com/PaulPhaneuf

Personal Website: www.PaulPhaneuf.com

Book Website: www.SovereignUnderGod.com

ADVOCACY & WATCHDOG GROUPS

Accuracy in Media

www.aim.org

Americans for Limited Government

www.getliberty.org/

Americans for Prosperity

www.americansforprosperity.org/

Americans for Tax Reform

www.atr.org/

Citizens against Government Waste

www.cagw.org/

Fact Check

www.factcheck.org

FreedomWorks

www.freedomworks.org/

NRA - National Rifle Association

www.NRA.org

NumbersUSA

www.numbersusa.com

Media Research Center

www.mrc.org/

Second Amendment Foundation

www.saf.org

Tax Foundation

www.taxfoundation.org/

BOOKS

David Barton – **ORIGINAL INTENT: THE COURTS, THE CONSTITUTION, AND RELIGION,** WallBuilder Press, Aledo, Texas, 1996

Frederick Bastiat – **THE LAW,** Foundation For Economic Education, Atlanta, 2007

Milton Friedman – **CAPITALISM AND FREEDOM,** University of Chicago Press, 2002

Barry Goldwater – **THE CONSCIENCE OF A CONSERVATIVE**, Regnery Publishing, 1994

W. Cleon Skousen - **THE 5,000 YEAR LEAP**, National Center for Constitutional Studies, 2007

F. A. Hayek – **THE ROAD TO SERFDOM**: Text and Documents--The Definitive Edition (The Collected Works of F. A. Hayek, Volume 2), University of Chicago Press, 2007

Henry Hazlitt – **ECONOMICS IN ONE LESSON**: The Shortest and Surest Way to Understand Basic Economics, Three Rivers Press, 1988

Ron Paul – **END THE FED**, Grand Central Publishing, 2009

Ayn Rand - Ayn Rand Box Set: **ATLAS SHRUGGED**/ **THE FOUNTAINHEAD**, Signet (2009)

R.J. Rummel – **DEATH BY GOVERNMENT**, Transaction Publishers, 1997

Larry Schweikart & Michael Allen – **A PATRIOT'S HISTORY OF THE UNITED STATES**, Sentinel Trade, 2007

Thomas Sowell – **ECONOMIC FACTS AND FALLACIES**, Basic Books, NY, 2011

Henry David Thoreau – **CIVIL DISOBEDIENCE**, Thoreau Classics, 2013

CHRISTIAN SITES & BOOKS

American Center for Law and Justice - ACLJ

www.aclj.org

American Family Association

www.afa.net

C.S. Lewis - **MERE CHRISTIANITY**, Harper San Francisco, 2009

Josh McDowell - **THE NEW EVIDENCE THAT DEMANDS A VERDICT FULLY UPDATED TO ANSWER THE QUESTIONS CHALLENGING CHRISTIANS TODAY**, Thomas Nelson, 1999

National Organization for Marriage

www.NationForMarriage.org

National Right to Life

www.nrlc.org

WallBuilders (David Barton)

www.wallbuilders.com

EDUCATIONAL WEBSITES

Ayn Rand Institute

www.aynrand.org/

American Enterprise Institute

www.aei.org

Atlas Network

www.atlasnetwork.org

Constitution Society

www.constitution.org

Constitution 101 – Free from Hillsdale College

www.constitution.hillsdale.edu

Ludwig von Mises Institute

www.mises.org

Heritage Foundation

www.heritage.org

Hoover Institution

www.hoover.org

Project Vote Smart

www.votesmart.org

FOUNDING DOCUMENTS

Declaration of Independence

www.constitution.org/us_doi.htm

United States Constitution

www.constitution.org/us_doi.htm

State Constitutions

    www.constitution.org/cons/usstcons.htm

Primary Source Documents

    www.constitution.org/primarysources/primarysources.html

GOVERNMENT INFORMATION

Library of Congress

    www.loc.gov/

The White House

    www.whitehouse.gov

United States Senate

    www.senate.gov

United States Congress

    www.house.gov

LIBERTARIAN

Advocates for Self Government

    www.theadvocates.org

CATO Institute

    www.cato.org

Foundation for Economic Education

    www.fee.org

International Society for Individual Liberty

www.isil.org

Reason Foundation

www.reason.org

PATRIOT ORGANIZATIONS

Oath Keepers

www.oathkeepers.org

Veterans of Foreign Wars

www.vfw.org

American Legion

www.legion.org

TEA PARTY WEB SITES

Tea Party Groups by State

www.teaparty911.com/info/locations.htm

Tea Party Meetup Groups

www.tea-party.meetup.com/

TeaParty.net

TeaPartyNation.com

TeaPartyPatriots.org

Dedication

To my father Emile Phaneuf, who passed May 5, 1999 and who in WWII served in the Asian theater;

To my uncle Albert Phaneuf who served in the Navy, deceased;

To my mother's brothers, my uncles Roland and Aram Grimard who each earned a Silver Star at the Battle of the Bulge, and my uncle Edmond Grimard who served as a mine sweeper in the navy, all deceased;

And to all those who came before and passed to us the legacy of liberty;

To those among my friends and family who have and do now risk life and limb, and who shall remain unnamed herein so that only I shall bare responsibility and consequences for my words;

To those who gave their all;

To my children, my grandchildren and the generations to come;

To those to whom in each generation the torch is passed and who choose to carry it forward;

We are resolved that we have not labored in vain who fought and will always fight for freedom's gain...

Paul Phaneuf

Acknowledgements

When you write a book you begin to relate to the truth that you rarely do anything of worth alone.

To those who have helped me complete this project I am grateful. There are too many people to name who have been engaged in the enterprise of Liberty and with whom I have battled the enemies of freedom. You know who you are. You have my respect and gratitude.

Jeanne and Dennis Champagne, my thanks for your input, proofreading, feedback and support...

Emile Phaneuf, for your proofreading and suggestions; we march on for a cause that is larger than ourselves...

My brother Ray with whom I have been engaged in the battle for decades...

Kathy Hauser: thank you for your input and invaluable editing contributions. You helped make this a better book...

My wife Yvonne who has heard everything I think and talk about a thousand times and who has allowed me the latitude to be who I am, at great personal cost to herself; for your love and commitment I thank God daily. We have paid the price together and it has been great, to pursue what to many is nothing but an empty exercise in futility.

For the sake of our children and grandchildren, we will prove the scoffers to be wrong.

In the final analysis, the errors and content are my responsibility alone. I stand on what I have written and I make no apologies.

Paul Phaneuf

Endnotes

---

[1] Signer of the Declaration of Independence

[2] The reader will find that "liberty" and "Liberty" are used throughout the book. I admit that often the distinction is arbitrary. I have intermittently capitalized Liberty because in my own mind it is both a description of a condition of freedom among men as well as a virtue and gift to men from their Creator. Both are important and I intermittently capitalized Liberty to highlight this concept.

[3] Throughout this book I refer to "man" in the generic sense of "humankind". Humankind is clearly man and woman. The construct is for ease of reading.

[4] Declaration of Independence

[5] Romans 9:21

[6] Isaiah 1:18

[7] Proverbs 27:17

[8] Libertinism is the deliberate disregard of moral restraints. It is liberty without responsibility, without regard for consequences, or concern for how our actions impact our fellow man. Freedom cannot be unlimited. We have all heard the saying that my rights end where yours begin.

Paul Phaneuf

---

⁹ 1 Timothy 6:10

¹⁰ Declaration of Independence

¹¹ Preamble to the Constitution of the United States

¹² As that was several decades ago, things have changed. I would like to expand my thoughts about radical Islam because it relates to my question of knowing what you believe and why you believe it and how that impacts our freedom.

The twenty first century brings a unique threat to our way of life because of the incursion of an antithetical worldview that eviscerates the freedom of thought and the individual liberty that is central to our Judeo Christian paradigm. Furthermore, while it is vital to defend and protect ourselves from this violent extremism, we must be on high alert as our government does what governments always do: accrues illegitimate power to itself in the name of national defense.

Since 9/11/2001, media attention has exposed radical Islam, particularly Sharia, as so irrational that it is not only not relatable, it is repulsive; killing yourself and innocents for Allah as the only sure way to get to heaven; beheading infidels; shooting teenage girls in the head because they want to go to school; beating women because their ankles are exposed; "honor" killings where fathers murder their own daughters.

I have since read numerous books about Islam written by Muslims and former Muslims. Most Muslims are reasonable and reject the lunacy of radical jihads and the extremes of Sharia. Sensible people are not attracted to radical Islam; they are driven to it by the sword of conquest, hence its militant theocratic fanaticism. To my mind, radical Islam is not rational and it cannot be true because God is not insane.

The barbarism of Sharia with its degradation of women, in and of itself, is an existential threat to our unalienable rights and our very lives. Mobs of programmed lunatics who demand that we restrict our First Amendment freedoms are a grave threat. However, this threat carries within it the seeds of excess as it obscures overreaching by our own government and distracts us from restricting the growth of the power of the beast among us.

As free men, this increases the danger to us on two fronts. We must be diligent.

[13] I refer to God as "He" because I am a Christian and that is how Jesus tells us to pray to God (Mat 6:9 NASB) "Pray, then, in this way: 'Our Father who is in heaven, Hallowed be Your name...'"

[14] Francis Schaeffer, <u>He Is There And He Is Not Silent</u>, Tyndale Press, 1972

[15] Psalm 19:1

[16] Romans 1:20

[17] Genesis 1:26

[18] Exodus 20:1-3

[19] Mark 12:17

[20] Deuteronomy 10:14; Psalm 24:1; Psalm 50:10, Psalm 50:12; 1 Chronicles 29:11; Colossians 1:16

²¹ American Pledge of Allegiance [brackets] are the author's personal comments

²² "Death By Government" R.J. Rummel, see Resources to order from Amazon

²³ Micah 6:8

²⁴ Mark 9:35

²⁵ Hebrews 12:1

²⁶ Exodus 18:21

²⁷ Galatians 5:1

²⁸ Mathew 7:7; Luke 11:9;

²⁹ Isaiah 33:22

³⁰ Galatians 5:13

³¹ 1Peter 2:16

³² Psalm 119:45

³³ Isaiah 61:1

³⁴ James 2:12

³⁵ Matthew 22:37-39

³⁶ Preamble to the United States Constitution; [brackets] are the author's personal comments

³⁷ Preamble to the Bill of Rights; [brackets] are the author's personal comments

---

[38] Articulated in the Declaration of Independence

[39] First Amendment, Bill of Rights; [brackets] are the author's personal comments

[40] Second Amendment, Bill of Rights

[41] Fourth Amendment, Bill of Rights

[42] Fifth Amendment, Bill of Rights

[43] Sixth and Seventh Amendments, Bill of Rights

[44] As to fact: Seventh Amendment; as to law: common law, common sense, law of conscience; de facto reality that no judge can overturn a not guilty verdict, nor may anyone be tried twice for the same offense; this interpretation has been confirmed by numerous writings of the Founders.

[45] John Adams: "It is not only his right, but his duty...to find the verdict according to his own best understanding, judgment and conscience, though in direct opposition to the direction of the court."

[46] Ninth Amendment, Bill of Rights

[47] Color of law is what you get when you ignore real Law, e.g. it's wrong to steal, and substitute it with fake statutes that everyone pretends is real law, such as An Act by Congress Number Blabber-Blabber signed by President Such and Such. "Heretofore and ever after it shall be known that we the Congress have decided that we are smarter than God and therefore and forevermore it shall be legal for us to take from you because we've decided that it is charitable for us to give your property to someone we've decided deserves it more than you be-

cause you are a greedy pig and wouldn't know what to do with it anyway. (Or else.)" You can substitute any nonsense you want here because once the line is crossed, there are no limits to what our servant government can do to us in the name of whatever they choose. If the freedom given us by our Creator, and the Laws of Nature and Nature's God, and the chains of the Constitution won't stop them, if not us, what do you think will?

[48] Genesis 1:26, 28

[49] Romans 13, 1Peter 2

[50] Matthew 6:23

[51] US Constitution, Article I, Section 8, Clause 6

[52] John Adams: "All the perplexities, confusion and distress in America arise not from defects in their Constitution or Confederation, nor from want of honor or virtue, so much as downright ignorance of the nature of coin, credit and circulation."

[53] Abraham Lincoln: "The money powers prey upon the nation in times of peace and conspire against it in times of adversity. It is more despotic than a monarchy, more insolent than autocracy, and more selfish than bureaucracy. It denounces as public enemies, all who question its methods or throw light upon its crimes. I have two great enemies, the Southern Army in front of me and the Bankers in the rear. Of the two, the one at my rear is my greatest foe. Corporations have been enthroned and an era of corruption in high places will follow, and the money powers of the country will endeavor to prolong its reign by working upon the prejudices of the

people until the wealth is aggregated in the hands of a few, and the Republic is destroyed."

54 Time Magazine cover asked on April 8, 1966, "Is God Dead?"

55 Thomas Jefferson: Papers, 334 (C.J. Boyd, Ed., 1950) "... God forbid we should ever be twenty years without such a rebellion. The people cannot be all, and always, well informed. The part which is wrong will be discontented, in proportion to the importance of the facts they misconceive. If they remain quiet under such misconceptions, it is lethargy, the forerunner of death to the public liberty.... And what country can preserve its liberties, if its rulers are not warned from time to time, that this people preserve the spirit of resistance? Let them take arms. The remedy is to set them right as to the facts, pardon and pacify them. What signify a few lives lost in a century or two? The tree of liberty must be refreshed from time to time, with the blood of patriots and tyrants. It is its natural manure."

56 The Patriot Act; the 2011 & 2012 Defense Authorization Act has provisions to use the military domestically, to detain American citizens. The Posse Comitatus Act of 1878 which prevents the military from engaging in law enforcement on United States territory has been repealed.

57 Bastiat in <u>The Law</u> develops this line of thought masterfully.

58 Preamble to the Bill of Rights

59 Preamble to the Constitution of the United States

[60] Matthew 6:24

[61] Mark 14:7

[62] John 8:32

[63] John 3:16

[64] Galatians 3:13

[65] Ephesians 2:8-9

[66] Romans 8:1